THE WIDE WORLD
MY PARISH

THE WIDE WORLD MY PARISH

Salvation and its Problems

YVES CONGAR, O.P.

Translated by
Donald Attwater

HELICON PRESS
BALTIMORE

HELICON PRESS INC.

1120 N. CALVERT ST.

BALTIMORE 2, MARYLAND

Library of Congress Catalog Card Number 61–14675

English translation first published 1961
© *Darton, Longman & Todd Ltd., 1961*
Reprinted 1962

First published in France by Témoignage
Chrétien, Paris, under the title
Vaste Monde, ma Paroisse

234
COW

'I look upon the world as my parish.'

John Wesley

CONTENTS

Preface

Christians have simultaneously become newly conscious of their minority position in the world and of the absolutely universal character of God's 'plan'. At a time when this minority position and the daily pressure of Communism are in a measure driving them to take their faith really seriously, and when the liturgical movement and the biblical renewal are giving them back a sense of the Lord's total absolute sovereignty, at this moment they are also strongly experiencing the call of a world that has to be built up. Their looking upward to God is being strengthened and refined; at the same time, when they look about them, they see so many different people amongst whom they have to live, with whom they have to enter into relation and to co-operate in this work of making the world.

For thoughtful people, the problems of salvation, and of the salvation of 'the others', have thus become a constant subject of inquiry. They keep on coming back to the questions that are put to us clergy. In this little book we are trying to provide some elements of the answers.

We do not conceal their incompleteness. A full answer would require the setting out of a complete theology of salvation, and therefore of the redemption too; it would be necessary to deal step by step with the fall, with sin, with God's plan, with the mystical body, with the problem of evil, with death. But to do this would have been to go far beyond the limits of this little book (which originated in a series of articles for *Témoignage Chrétien*), and to exceed the little time left to us by other tasks. But we are painfully conscious of all that is missing from the answers herein if anyone were to take them for a full explanation. In particular, much is omitted in respect of the specific teachings of dogma; and these deficiencies should be supplied by reference to more markedly catechetical works, preferably the Catechism itself, which is the best over-all synthesis of the Catholic faith.[1]

The answers given in this book take the questions on their own ground, as they are asked; the problems are approached more from the side of man and of the world. But these aspects are not foreign either to Catholic tradition or to its source, holy Scripture.

However, even from this side the problems go considerably beyond the area of the questions considered here. We have not even touched on any of the cosmic problems confronted by, for example, Father Teilhard de Chardin. Were the matter to be treated fully, the chapter on 'the others' would have to give more attention to the problems of 'dialogue' and living together. The divided world in which we live requires that we should be very careful to maintain the integrity of our attitudes, but it ought also to be a world of exchange of ideas and co-operation. So there ought to be sections of this chapter headed Oecumenism, Conditions for 'pluralism' and human co-operation in a spiritually-divided world, Tolerance, Possibility of a 'Christian politics', and so forth.

Sufficient unto the day is the task thereof. We have set out only to reply to the questions which have been directly put to us. I hope that the reader will be so kind as to take these pages

---

[1] For English-speaking readers mention may be made of Cardinal Gasparri's *The Catholic Catechism* (London, 1934); F. H. Drinkwater, *Abbreviated Catechism with Explanations* (Burns Oates, England and St Martin's Press, U.S.A., 1951); J. Kilgallon & G. Weber, *Christ in us* (London & New York, 1958); and *A Catholic Catechism* (Burns Oates, England and Herder, U.S.A., 1960). The last of these is the English edition of the new official German catechism, drawn up in line with today's biblical renewal and Christocentric approach. An excellent short work is E. Joly's *What is Faith?* (Burns Oates, 1958, Faith and Fact series; Hawthorne, Twentieth Century Encyclopaedia).

for what they are, without asking them to supply what we are humbly conscious is not there.

This book is strictly enough limited from yet another side, if indeed it can be said that Jesus Christ really puts a limit to anything. The questions treated here are raised in *Christian* terms, and their answers are outlined in *Christian* terms, starting from *Christian* premises. Many of them indeed are almost meaningless apart from such premises, which, given by the faith, are centred in Jesus Christ, in Christ confessed as God, as Saviour and as Lord. The faith teaches that God has a design for the world, that the world has a meaning, that Jesus Christ is the absolute of this design and this meaning.

Is that as much as to say that unbelievers can find nothing of interest in these *Christian* answers? To think that would be to give too little credit both to their open-mindedness and to the power of the Gospel. Those who today are searching the Scriptures for an answer to very great problems are by no means confined to the ranks of formal believers. Many people are groping and searching for him whom we have to tell them about (cf. Acts xvii. 23, 27). In any case, unbelievers can find interest, both for themselves and because of the dialogue they need to pursue with us, in learning what Christians think about such massive problems as the meaning of the world and its future in eternity.

One does not take the risk of entering into a dialogue—a book is one form of this risk—unless one has some guarantee of friendship and trust. I approach you, my unknown reader, in Christian friendship and in full human trustingness. You already have a place in my prayers before ever you open this little book, and so before we have met.

Strasbourg,   Y.C.
24 September 1959.

I

This New World We Live In . . .

WHEN we look at the questions that are discussed among Catholics today we find that very many of them bear on a clearly defined subject: they are concerned with the salvation of 'the others', with the relationship of other religions to Catholicism, with what happens after death, the number of the saved, the problem of evil, and, more dogmatically, with Purgatory and Hell. In other words, these questions raise the problem of the relation of the Catholic Church's definite teaching about salvation and its conditions with all that we know of the huge world which stretches far beyond the boundaries of Christianity, and even more of Catholicism.

WHY WAS CHRIST SO LONG IN COMING?

The world of the past, which may be called on the whole that of the middle ages or of Christendom, had the good fortune (if it was good) to see human culture in perfect agreement with what was said by the Christian religion. There is nothing surprising about that. Culture was in the hands of the clergy, and was a product of the Church through and through. For instance, the history of mankind appeared to be set out exactly in the chronology and surroundings that were found in the Bible. Even today, in the grand passage from the Roman Martyrology that is read at Christmas, the liturgy announces Christ's birth in the terms that in past ages everyone took to be literally exact: 'In the 5199th year of the creation of the world . . ., the 2957th year after the Flood, the 2015th year from Abraham's birth . . .' and the rest. It was firmly believed that at the time of Jesus Christ the world was little more than 5,000 years old. The rise and fall of empires seemed to fit exactly into the framework of the prophet Daniel's four empires (Dan. ii. 37ff.). Just consider how far we are from such ideas now.

Suppose a century of time to be represented by three seconds, and that Christ was born in some year exactly at midnight on 31 December. We now know that in accordance with this the beginnings of life would have to be dated on 1 January in that year, the appearance of the first marine vertebrates on 23 July and of the big reptiles on 20 October, the beginning of the quaternary age on 31 December at 2 o'clock p.m., and that of Neanderthal man at 7.32 p.m., and of the polished stone age at 11.55 p.m., both on this same date. According to this scheme, Abraham would be born on 31 December too, at about 11.59 p.m. As for the founding of Rome, four centuries before Christ, it would be dated 31 December, at some twelve seconds before midnight. . . .

In the early Church the Fathers[1] were already troubled by the question—which pagans did not fail to put on them—'Why did Christ come so late?' The answer that they gave, with their biblical culture and a chronology that is so ridiculously short for us, was that there had to be a time of preparation and that men needed to get used to the idea of God's coming. The question continued to haunt thoughtful people; and in our own day Charles Péguy wrote, in the first

---

[1] The Fathers of the Church were the great teachers who taught the faithful and fought false doctrine from the end of the apostolic age to about the end of the sixth century; e.g. St Athanasius (d. 373) in the East, St Augustine (d. 430) in the West. It was their vocation and gift to formulate the fundamental elements of Christian teaching in conjunction with the cultural heritage of antiquity, and for the Church they have the authority of great classical writers, preferred witnesses to her tradition.

Clio : 'That Jesus came into the world so late is one of the most difficult, baffling and agonizing of problems. Why should he be so long? Why did the God-man delay his entrance into human history?' Today it presents itself as a problem of reconciling the positive declarations of the Bible and Christianity with what we now know to be the extent of history and of the world. To a considerable degree this is what accounts for the success of certain writings which nevertheless also invite criticism, for example, those of Lecomte du Nouy and even, on a different plane of authority, those of Father Teilhard de Chardin.

Or again, consider our consciousness of the size and variety of this world of ours. Christian antiquity and the middle ages knew well enough that human beings existed beyond the frontiers of Christianity. But they were not interested in them, they did not have our driving curiosity to go and see what lay beyond the boundaries of the known world. This matter has been studied in relation to St Bernard (d. 1153);[1] and we find that he combined awareness that there were people outside the Christian world with a complete indifference to and an astonishing lack of concern about this 'beyond'. We should find it was the same with St Augustine or St Thomas Aquinas. And again we are quite different: if we come up against a barrier, we have an itch to get over it and to learn what is on the other side. We have done it for this planet, and we are not satisfied: our 'other side' is now outer space.

This change of attitude did not happen in a day; it took many centuries to come about. First there were the great discoveries, and the exchanging of old traditions as the ideal for the ideal of things new and strange. How significant is the inscription over the door of a chapel in the cathedral at Cahors: *Nove, nove, iterumque nove, nove :* 'The new, the new, again

[1] See P. Dérumaux, 'S. Bernard et les infidèles' in *Mélanges Saint Bernard* (Dijon, 1954), pp. 68–79.

3

and again the new!' That sentiment did not worry the cathedral canons at the end of the fifteenth century, but those of the twelfth or thirteenth would have been shocked by it.

There were not only the geographical, historical and intellectual discoveries of the sixteenth and seventeenth centuries; there was also the expansion of the Christian west to countries across the seas, first through missionaries and then traders and then soldiers. New peoples were discovered, and it was often found that these peoples had a civilization and a good moral standard, and were religious. In the first enthusiasm of these discoveries it was believed that many points of agreement could be established between these religions and Christianity; St Francis Xavier, for instance, thought he had found the Blessed Trinity and the Holy Family in Japanese religion. Later on it was realized that these religions were more different than at first believed, but that they nevertheless represented considerable positive approaches towards the mystery of the Godhead. Hence arose in the eighteenth century, more developed in the nineteenth, the comparative study of religions. But there also arose a number of problems touching the Christian faith, which can be summed up in what Ernest Troeltsch called the problem of the *absoluteness* of Christianity, which means these questions: In view of what the history of religions tells us about world religion, can it still be maintained that Christianity is absolute truth? What value is to be accorded to these different religions in relation to the Christian faith and the biblical revelation?

With the addition of critical difficulties raised by historical and philological study of the text of the Bible, such problems produced the crisis of Modernism at the end of the nineteenth century. Most modernists were moved by a desire to vindicate Christianity by reconciling science and religion, as they put it. But they were impatient, in too much of a hurry in their apologetics; and they also lacked a philosophy that was ade-

4

quate to deal with such questions. They often thought they had found the answer in a distinction that we today see to be superficial, if not disastrous: the distinction, that is, between *forms* that are relative and subject to all the changes and chances of history, and a *spirit* that is lasting, which alone can claim the soul's adherence. It is better understood today that it is form that safeguards spirit; and on numerous points criticism itself has justified the acceptance of positions which the modernists in their haste were glad to abandon.

WE, AND THE OTHERS

These problems raised by the development of knowledge have become more acute than ever today because the contemporary mind is so enormously taken up with man and his destiny. I should like here to refer to an idea put forward by St Robert Bellarmine, in the preface to his famous *Controversies*, the work in which he vindicated Catholic teaching against the Protestant reformers. In his review of the historical sequence of heresies, he saw them as pretty closely following the order of the articles in the Creed. First, he said, there were heresies about God, creator of all things, visible and invisible (Manicheism); then there were those about the Trinity (Arianism); and then those bearing on the Godhead of the incarnate Word (Nestorius, Monophysism); in the ninth century, attack was made on the doctrine of the Holy Spirit. The heresies of his own time, Bellarmine pointed out, bore on the Church, the communion of saints, remission of sin, justification—and there he stopped: it was the year 1582. Cannot we add that in our time questioning or error is more especially concerned with the last article in the Creed, everlasting life and the world to come? Modern man is less interested in God than in what is going to happen to himself, in his salvation, to use the Christian word.

Then, too, many contemporary currents of thought are

powerfully concerned about 'the others'. It is not for nothing that so many people are interested in what is called Ecumenism. A man cannot content himself with the certain knowledge that the Catholic Church represents the fullness of Christianity (supposing that he has that certainty unimpaired); he needs to know what 'the others' represent in relation to that Church and the salvation of which she is as it were the sacrament. In many places, every Catholic knows people who are Protestant, perhaps a communist or two, maybe a Jew, and certainly some who 'don't care', either because of indifference or because they are positively opposed to religion. These people are his fellows, sharing a common destiny with him, and he, or she, cannot but ask how they stand with regard to his religion, his faith, and that salvation in which he believes. The Communism pervading some countries, which has imposed some of its problems on us, is in its own way underlining the question: on the one hand by the atmosphere of human solidarity and ever-growing 'worldwideness'; on the other, by consciousness of a tremendous historical continuity which forbids us to ignore the solidarity of generation with generation and century with century. It may be that the religion of the classical epoch was characterized by a certain individualism: Peter Nicole (d. 1695), for example, declared that 'A man is created to live alone with God for ever.' A possible comment on this nowadays is one that would have astonished and even scandalized Nicole: 'Save my own soul alone? No; it shall be all or none!' Whilst not going so far as that, this feeling for human solidarity certainly haunts many Christian consciences today.[1]

[1] This feeling could be particularly illustrated from the writings of Simone Weil, but there are much older expressions of it, though inspired by different considerations. There is Dostoevsky's theme that we are responsible for all people and everything, we have to beg forgiveness for all people and everything; and St Simeon the New Theologian (d. 1022) wrote; 'I knew a man who so longed for his brethren's salvation that, with excess of a zeal worthy of Moses, he implored God with scalding tears that either those brethren should be saved with him or he be damned with

SO MANY QUESTIONS!

In face of such a consciousness, to try to keep the faithful in a sort of Catholic ghetto, cut off from the outside world and in ignorance of the interests and upheavals of human society, is a positively fantastic idea. And recent popes have not spoken in favour of any such thing: Pius XII especially called on Catholics again and again boldly to take their part in the world's affairs, and obviously that means that they come into contact with 'the others'.[1] That once more raises problems for them.

The most certain conclusions of contemporary philosophical thought point in exactly the same direction. They show us that the structure of the human intellect involves 'dialogue', discussion. Intellect is made to deal with what is universal, and it requires 'give and take', to be exercised in contact with the intellects of others. Dialogue inevitably entails risks which ignorance is spared—but ignorance has its difficulties too! In our day, the Christian has more than ever to be a soldier of Christ, and therefore vigorous and strong. If he is to keep up with the world in which he is called to live and bear witness, the first effort required of him is almost everywhere an effort of the mind, the intellect, of intelligence and understanding.

---

them. For he was bound to them in the Holy Spirit by such a bond of love that he did not want even to enter the kingdom of Heaven if it meant having to be separated from them' (Discourse 22; P.G., 120, 424–5).

[1] For some of the relevant quotations, see Y. Congar, *Lay People in the Church* (London and Westminster, Md., 1957), pp. 444–6.

7

2

A Small Church in a Large World

IN countries which have an age-long tradition of Christianity
the Catholic Church, in varying degrees, has a place of
importance and also a kind of conspicuousness. We are continually meeting her in her buildings and other monuments, in
her clergy, in signs or traces of her influence. She is present
everywhere, and gives her members the feeling of belonging
to a very big thing. In certain lands she is particularly in evidence: whoever has been to Rome knows how the Church
and the Papacy dominate the scene.

But if, instead of going to Rome, we go, say, to the Scandi-
navian countries or to those of the Near East, such as Egypt
or Turkey, how different things are. There the Church seems
a very minor affair, and one sometimes has to pry about to
find any sign of her. Think of Tel Aviv in Palestine, a town of
170,000 inhabitants without a single Christian place of worship. And what about the huge countries, with millions and
millions of people in them, over great areas of which the Church
is simply not to be found at all? Recall that, in the middle of
this twentieth century, nearly one man in every four is Chinese,
and then ask yourself what place the Church has in China, what
does she look like there, what signs are there of her presence?

We often read fine accounts of distant foreign missions,
and some of them might well appear under the title 'When the
Spirit blows like a gale'. But when we study the statistics, we

are forced to admit that every year the proportion of heathen
in the world is growing in relation to that of Catholics. The
annual increase of Catholics through new births is about
3½ million; add half a million or so converts, and the total
increase is in the region of 4 million each year. But during
that time births have increased the number of non-Catholics
by over 16 million. Simply to maintain the present numerical
proportion there would have to be, not a half-million conver-
sions to Catholicism a year, but 6½ million. How far we are
from that was expressly recognized by Pius XII in his encyclical letter *Evangelii praecones* (1951).

We cannot but ask ourselves what these facts mean. And,
in this age of religious sociology and statistics, it is a good
thing to deepen our judgement somewhat by inquiring what
these figures signify with regard to faith, itself enlightened by
the word of God. 'A small church in a very large world': that
is a fact; what have faith and the Bible to say about it?

THE BIBLE AND STATISTICS

It is not intended to do more here than to sketch an answer
to our questions from a purely religious and theological standpoint, which is a thing rarely done. It is perhaps worth while
attempting it.

The biblical attitude to questions of number as affecting
God's people seems to be summarized in these two statements:
(1) The Bible looks on censuses of population in two different
ways; (2) the Bible shows little interest in the quantitative
aspects of things.

(1) Sometimes God himself ordered that the people be
numbered, and so no other justification was needed; this is
what happened at the beginning and towards the end of the
exodus from Egypt (Num. i. 19ff.; xiv. 29ff.). But see what
happened when David, having rounded off his kingdom and
brought peace to its borders, undertook to number his people:

the Bible sees in this a *temptation* to which David had given way (2 Kings xxiv. cf. 1 Paral. xxi; xxvii. 23–24). It seems that in carrying out this census David had aimed at finding out to what extent God had fulfilled his promise so far; and therefore it was an act of pride, or evidence of a lack of complete trust in God, of not leaving himself wholly in his hands. Moreover, David's punishment was visited on the people whose wealth and strength he wanted to gauge. The lesson of this significant fact is that God's people must not be treated as a merely quantitative thing; where that people is concerned it must never be considered entirely without reference to faith, as if it were just any social group.

(2) It is disconcerting to notice how often numbers given in the Bible do not mean just the same as numbers mean for us. It happens quite often that, in parallel accounts, the figures given in one do not agree with those given in the other. David's census just referred to is a case in point. Biblical exegetes have a ready answer: they tell us that there were several different sources and editors. But the difficulty remains; for the final editor or whoever gathered the sources, who was no more stupid than we are, must have noticed that the figures were different, and yet he left them. They cannot then have had the same importance or exactly the same meaning for him as for us. In many other passages numbers have a symbolical signification, and on these the Fathers and specialists in typology have been able to exercise the ingenuity of their minds. Or again, sometimes numbers are arranged according to a certain idea, to convey some meaning, or even for the sake of symmetry and balance in the context: a good example is the genealogy of Jesus as set out by St Matthew, who groups the generations in three series of fourteen. There is another example in the figures of the members of Jacob's family who came into Egypt, the total of whom has been so arranged as to make seventy, a mystic number.

These, and numerous other examples that could be given, show how little interest the Bible has in a quantitative aspect as such. What, then, is its point of view?

THE FEW WHO REPRESENT THE WHOLE

The fundamental biblical category is not quantity but rather the idea of representative elements having a universal dynamic value; these features are found in the typically biblical notion of first-fruits. 'Biblical thought is all-embracing, it includes the particular in the whole, whether as seed, root or fruit of a tree' (W. Vischer). We must look at this more closely.

First of all, the Bible is not concerned with numbers as such, but with the fact that a number of individuals actualize the characteristics of the real type that governs and precedes them: we have only to consider what the Old Testament says of Edom and Israel respectively. The New Testament is interested in the *totalities* which are deemed to be present in a representative *part* of each. So, for instance, the Devil shows Jesus '*all* the kingdoms of the world' (Matt. iv. 8); at the moment of his return to Heaven, our Lord gives his apostles the mission to make disciples 'of *all* nations' (*ib*. xxviii. 19). St Paul often speaks in this way. He refers to 'the gospel which has been preached to *all* creation under heaven' (Col. i. 23); the Jerusalem Bible suggests that this is only an hyperbole, but surely there is something else in it as well. Paul also writes 'the gospel which has reached you, which now bears fruit and thrives in you, as it does *all* the world over' (Col. i. 5–6), and he speaks elsewhere of 'Achaia' and of 'Macedonia'. His biographer, St Luke, says in the same way that Paul taught for two years at Ephesus 'so that the Lord's word came to the ears of *all* those who lived in Asia, both Jews and Greeks' (Acts xix. 10). These pointers might seem insignificant were it not for the fact that they form part of a whole context, well known to specialists, in which the idea of totality is very strongly marked.

But this totality is considered as represented in a *part* of itself, which is the bearer, according to God's 'plan', of the destiny of the whole. Such biblical studies as those of Wilhelm Vischer show that this dynamic and continuous plan is characterized by the idea of *Pars pro toto*, a part for the whole. Mankind is chosen to represent the world, to give God the praise of all creation; Israel is chosen for mankind, to be God's witness and priest amongst men, and at bottom the Jewish people has maintained its consciousness of this vocation and ideal as the indelible mark of its chosenness, even when it has fallen short of its call: 'A minority in the service of a majority.'[1] But for us Israel is now the Church, and it is to Christians that we have to apply the idea of being the dynamic representative minority that is spiritually responsible for the final destiny of all.

Even within Israel a part often stood for the whole. When the more fervent Jews were gathered at Jerusalem for the great feasts, it was *all* Israel that was, mystically, assembled there. When, from the eighth century B.C., the prophets began to foretell the destruction of the Holy City and its Temple, they spoke prophetically of 'the remnant', whose size was of little importance and was not made clear, but which would represent the whole of the new Israel. Finally, the new Israel is represented and has its points of departure, not in a collective remnant, but in one person, the Son of Man, who bears in himself all the Holy People of the Most High. Fundamentally,

---

[1] J. Guitton says of Bergson: 'His thought is paralleled by the very Jewish idea of mankind's development coming about through the choice of a branch, a branch that flourishes when the tree withers. God chose Abraham, and then he chose again from among Abraham's descendants. Mankind is saved by a *small remnant*. It is the same in Bergson's evolutionary idea. The life-force (*élan vital*) is smothered in vegetable torpor, in animal instinct, in the mechanization of many societies and of closed minds, only to appear among mystics, and among the only "complete mystics" of Catholicism.' (*Mémorial J. Chaine*, Lyons, 1950, p. 201, n. 9.)

the Christian doctrine of the Redemption cannot be understood apart from the biblical idea of representative inclusion of which a few examples have just been given. It is indeed constantly 'a part for the whole': God looked at a great multitude and brought them into his design, seeing them in a little group or in a single person who providentially was bearer of the good that was meant for all.

THE SEED OF LIFE

That is why we said above that the ideas of totality and of representative value are joined in the typically biblical notion of first-fruits. The apostolic writings are full of it. According to St James' epistle, Christians, to whom birth is given by the Father through his true word, are the first-fruits of all his creation (i. 18). For St Paul, Christ is the first-fruits of resurrection (1 Cor. xv. 20, 23); and Stephanas and his fellows are the first-fruits of Achaia (1 Cor. xvi. 15), Epaenetus of Asia (Rom. xvi. 5). Clearly Paul saw in the first of a group or a country an example of the divine pattern according to which that first contains all that is to follow. The idea can be applied to the founder of some group, e.g. of a church or a religious order, or of a Catholic Action organization, such as the Young Christian Workers. We are now such rabid individualists that ideas of this sort no longer occur to us; and yet, even humanly speaking, we should not be what we are, or rather, we should not be at all, had there not been a First in whom the future was contained. In one of his sermons, Newman has a fine passage on the bond that unites us with our forerunners, of whom we often know nothing but to whom we nevertheless owe things that are very dear and precious to us.[1] Who built the house in which we were born and grew up? Who began the society in which we have found opportunity and happiness, human or specifically Christian? In biblical language all

---

[1] *Parochial Sermons*, vol. iii (London, 1836), Sermon 17.

these things would be 'first-fruits'; but here we have to go beyond the purely human point of view.

We all know that for Christians, there is a real history of salvation: that is, a chain of events and divine dealings in accordance with a design seen by God in its wholeness from all eternity, but which is unfolded bit by bit during the course of time. To the eyes of God, its continuation was in its beginning, he saw the whole in the first-fruits. For God, Abraham, alone in a world that was already populous, was already the people that would make up the company of believers; the promises and blessings given to the patriarch were given for this people. Thus Abraham in his solitude was as it were a seed that was able to fertilize the field of the world, a kind of sacrament of universal faith and salvation.

And do we not see there a sort of general law, a 'constant' of all creation? With deep penetration did Gustave Thibon write that 'Any order that transcends another can insert itself into that other only under a form that is infinitely small'; he gives as examples the insertion of life into the inorganic world and of the power of thought into simply biological life; to which may be added, of the Church's supernatural life into the world of conscious life. And indeed, what is life, quantitatively considered, in face of the enormous mass of lifeless matter? It is so small in relation to the mass as to be hardly perceptible, and yet it is the promise and the riches and the future.

The same can be said of conscious life in relation to life in general. Pascal's reed is a well-known symbol,[1] but it does not speak so persuasively as figures, and here are the figures: It has been calculated that if the whole population of the world were put into the Lake of Geneva, which is not all that large, the level of the water would rise by only $11\frac{1}{4}$ inches. That is a matter of bodies. But consciousness has neither density nor

---

[1] 'Man is only a reed, the weakest thing in nature; but he is a thinking reed' (*Pensées*, vi, 347).

volume nor weight, and yet it is the greatest thing in the world. And then what shall we say of grace, of which the Church is as it were the shrine? Here we may recall that fine piece, No 792, of Pascal's *Pensées*, on the three orders: the bodily order, the order of mind, and the order of charity or holiness.

The infinite distance between body and mind is a figure of the infinitely more infinite distance between mind and charity—for charity is supernatural.

The glory of greatness shines in vain for people who are in search of understanding.

Kings, the rich, public leaders, none of the great ones of the world see the glory of men of intellect.

The greatness of wisdom, which is nothing if not of God, is invisible to worldlings and intellectuals. These are three orders that differ in kind.

Great geniuses have their power, their glory, their greatness, their triumphs, their lustre, and have no need of worldly greatness, it is no concern of theirs. They are seen by the mind, not with the eyes; and that is enough.

The saints have their power, their glory, their triumphs, their lustre, and have no need of wordly or intellectual greatness, with which they have no concern, for these neither add to nor take away anything from them. They are seen by God and the angels, not by the body or by inquisitive minds; God is enough for them.

Archimedes would be equally revered whatever his place in the world. He fought no eye-filling battles, but he gave his discoveries to every man's mind. How glorious he was to the mind!

Jesus Christ, without wordly goods and without any outward show of learning, belongs to his own order of holiness. He did not invent anything, he did not govern; but he was humble, patient, holy, holy to God, terrifying to evil spirits, without sin. With how much state, with what unutterable splendour, he comes to the eyes of the heart that perceives wisdom!

It would have been useless for Archimedes to play the prince in his geometry books, though he was a prince.

15

It would have been useless for our Lord Jesus Christ to come like a king to dazzle us in his kingdom of holiness; he came indeed with the glory of his own order!

... All bodies together, and all minds together, and all their works, cannot equal the least movement of charity—that is of an infinitely higher order.

3

Jacob's Ladder

WE have seen that the Bible shows us God at work in the world according to a plan, raising up 'first-fruits', that is, a part representing a whole and having a universal power. And it is from this background that we must approach the problems which we want to examine with the eye of faith: Christianity and other religions, the salvation of unbelievers, and of those who have never heard of Christ's gospel. At the outset there are two ideas involved understanding of which is perhaps weak amongst us, but there are contemporary lines of thought that can help us to grasp them better: the ideas of *totality* and of *plan*.

There is a hallowed truth in 'personalism', the feeling for the unique value of every person; a person is a whole in himself, one cannot be substituted for another, he is the contrary of Koestler's definition of the individual in a communist society: 'A mass of one million people divided by a million.' But we must not lose sight of other truths. Every man and woman is a person, but they all have something else in common, their humanity. Mankind is made up of persons, but they are born one of another, they need one another in order to expand and develop, each one has his own destiny, but together they pursue a common cause: 'The whole succession of men should be seen as one and the same man, continuing always to exist and to learn.' The world too is a totality; science treats it more and more as a whole, made of the same stuff, and all held together by an aggregate of inter-actions, attractions and compenetrations.

The world as a whole has movement and therefore a mean-ing. Materialism treats this movement and meaning as purely a result of forces within nature, though adding that it is man's business to interpret them by his intelligence and to apply his energies to them. But from the Christian point of view the world as a whole has a meaning which comes to it from God's plan. Plan and meaning are not simply those which the mind can recognize by carefully looking at things. Into the world taken as a whole, into the pattern of human history, God put the revelation and then the gift of something new; it was not contained within the energies of the world but, once given, it became its central point and constituted its meaning: the Covenant, fully actualized in Jesus Christ who is indeed the union of God and man. Jesus is for the world, and the world is for Jesus: totality in quest of a meaning, and fullness of meaning. We cannot be sure that in Jesus Christ the world recognizes its meaning, but it is certain that he is that meaning.

Let me make a comparison. At one time I was living my life from day to day, and pretty happily, for my job was interesting. But, without having the sophisticated absurdity of Sartre's 'Everything that exists is born for no purpose, con-tinues through weakness, dies by chance', that life of mine was not illumined by the shining light of some clear purpose. Then one day I met somebody who put an idea into my head, something worth-while, an undertaking, in which I recog-nized *the* meaning of my life; it not only determined my present and future, but threw light on the past, for everything had been pointing in this direction, although I had not realized it. Taken up with living and doing my work, I had overlooked it, but even so it was the meaning of my life; it made sense of everything and held the whole together. Boris Pasternak is right: 'You have said that facts don't mean anything by themselves—not until a meaning is put into them. Well—the meaning you have to put into the facts to make them relevant to human beings is just that: it's Christianity, it's the mystery of personality.'

If then, this is the place of Jesus Christ, we have to determine what is the consequent place of the Church, in relation to him and in relation to the world.

The Church is Church only because of Christ, but she is made up of human beings. She is a gathering of men among other gatherings of men, but bearing amongst them the mystery of Jesus Christ. She is the company of witnesses to him. *In as much as it depends on men's faithfulness,* she brings Christ to the world, offering it opportunities to recognize him as the key to its destiny.

Provided we are careful not to turn a convenient and, surely, necessary distinction into a separation, it will be useful to look at the Church from each of two points of view: (1) as God's people, the community of Christians, she represents mankind towards Christ; (2) as institution, or sacrament of salvation, she represents Christ towards the world. Jacob 'dreamed that he saw a ladder standing on the earth, with its top reaching up into heaven; a stairway for the angels of God to go up and come down' (Gen. xxviii. 12; cf. John i. 51). Two mediations are joined in the Church, one going up, or representative, the other coming down, or sacramental; and through them she is the place where Christ gives himself to the world, and the world gives itself to Christ, the place where the two meet.

In this two-fold movement the Church actualizes the biblical idea of first-fruits. Coming from Christ and composed of men, she constantly bears the whole of one towards the whole of the other. When she takes root in some human grouping, there she makes Jesus Christ present and at work, that Son of

God of whom St Paul writes that it is God's pleasure 'through him to win back *all things*, whether on earth or in heaven, into union with himself, making peace with them through his blood, shed on the cross' (Col. i. 20). No doubt this does not mean that all men, in the sense of each and every individual, will in fact be saved; it means that the act by which Christ makes the union effective is of itself really directed towards and includes all men, the totality of the world as such, offering all that is necessary for the achievement of the end that God has in view for them.

Since the Church makes Jesus Christ present and active to the world, all worth is finally judged by her, and it is in regard to her that men are seen to be blessed or rejected. Clement of Alexandria had this in mind when he wrote, early in the third century, 'Just as God's will is a deed and it is called "the world", so his intention is man's salvation, and this is called "the Church".'[1] That is not plainly seen as physical things are: 'What do we see now? Not all things subject to him as yet' (Heb. ii, 8). What St Paul says of the Christian is not true of his personal life alone, but also of apostleship and of all that the Church does: 'Your life is hidden away now with Christ in God. Christ is your life, and when he is made manifest, you too will be made manifest in glory with him' (Col. iii. 3–4).

It is true that to the eye of faith the Church never looks small in this great world. There she wears the best aspect she can, for the people she is able to reach. But, however modestly,

[1] *Paedagogus*, i, 6. It is very remarkable that this idea, of bearing the world's meaning like a living seed, was given expression at the very time when Christians were a small minority, looked on with contempt, persecuted and often killed off. See also the *Letter to Diognetus* (2-cent.): 'Christians are in the world what the soul is in the body. The soul is dispersed throughout the members of the body, so are Christians among the cities of the world. . . . Christians are as it were held in the prison of the world; yet it is they who sustain the world.' St Irenaeus (d. *c*. 200) speaks of the 'recapitulation' of *all things* in Christ, the Church's head (cf. Eph. i. 10). Origen (d. *c*. 254) calls the Church 'the universe of the universe'. And so on.

she has always to seek to have and to show an appearance that *betokens* the Gospel, that *betokens* the Covenant, and a covenant that is in principle universal, for of that she is the sign and sacrament.

Each one of us for his own little world, all of us for the world at large—we are Jacob's ladder. The representative going up of mankind to God and the representative coming down of Jesus Christ to the world pass through us. The whole Church is sacramental and missionary, and so is each Christian in his degree. Each of the members of any group (e.g. a parish) that seeks Christ through the Church stands for the whole group. To what extent do they effectively aid the group in its journey to God? It cannot be known. But they are its first-fruits, a sheaf offered up, and they are intercessors for it: had there been ten righteous men in the city, God would have spared it (Gen. xviii. 32).

We can only look ahead, and so we cannot see anything, for there is nothing to see in the future, unless with the eyes of faith and hope. It has been rightly observed that mankind goes forward in its history backwards, because it only sees the road it has already travelled. When we reach the end, we shall see how the final results took shape in the beginnings, the first-fruits. And we shall give thanks.

The Church's two-fold office of mediation entails a condition of power and of mission that is co-extensive with her very existence. The Church exists in herself, as a sacred thing in the midst of the world, but she does not exist *for* herself: she has a mission to and a responsibility for the world. So at the Church's heart there is a sort of polarity, a tension or dialectic, which it is very important to understand. From the beginning Christians have been pulled in two directions, like someone hearing two calls at once. More exactly, they are thus pulled when they live their religion faithfully in its fullness, for if one call ousts or drowns the other the question arises how and on what terms unity can be had.

The first voice is that of another world. 'Be not conformed to this world,' urged St Paul (Rom. xii. 2). Were the Church to listen *only* to this call, she would become an association of the immaculate, a hand-picked group that would leave the world to its fate. She would be composed of people of the strictest practice, scrupulous in prayer and observances, sedulously cut off from the world, undisturbed by what happened to others.

The second voice is that of this world and its enthralling destiny, the call of other men and the salvation of other men. Were they to follow *only* this call, Christians would simply become ardent champions of Progress, of History, of all those things whose names are written with capital letters, which for many people are in effect the only gods they explicitly acknowledge. It would then look as if Christianity were *nothing else than* the inner meaning of the world and a means to the happiness of human beings (that has happened in certain schools of thought, such as the Christian Socialism of Frederick Denison Maurice in England).

Now Christianity is that, but *because* it is *something else* first. It has a mission to the world and embraces it; but in the first place it exists in itself, as an institution coming from Jesus Christ, a people which testifies to him. Grain is for seed-time and harvest, but it has to be brought together and it lives its own specific life.

According to the circumstances of the moment in the Church's history, Christians are more conscious now of one, now of her other aspect, the requirements of holiness or the calls of all-embracingness. The first Christian generations felt above all that they were the chosen ones, set apart from the world by knowledge and worship of the one true God. It would be very interesting to study from this point of view those early prayer texts that have come down to us, especially the eucharistic ones: that of the *Didache* (9–10), which goes back to the era of the Apostles, that of Clement of Rome (*Ep. Cor.* 59–61), who was an immediate disciple of the Apostles, that of Hippolytus (*Apost. Trad.*, 4), of the early third century. But when we get to Sarapion's great eucharistic prayer (Egypt, early fourth century) we find Christians first giving thanks for the gift of knowledge of God and for the salvation he had wrought for them, and then praying thus:

> Lover of man, lover of the poor, reconciler of all, whom you draw to yourself through the coming of your well-beloved Son, . . . make us men who have life. . . . Give us a holy spirit that we may be able to speak and tell your unutterable mysteries. Let Wisdom speak in us, and the Holy Spirit too. . . .

The Church's universal concern finds voice there, as it does i n the great intercession on Good Friday, in the litany of the saints, and, so profoundly and significantly, in the doxology that concludes the canon of the Mass: 'Through him and with him and in him are given to you, God the almighty Father, in the unity of the Holy Spirit, all honour and all glory. . . .' It is clear that at that moment we can and ought to make our double mediation supremely real, becoming a Jacob's ladder with Jesus himself (John i. 51) and in the Church.

At bottom, the Church and the world need one another. The Church means salvation for the world, but the world means health for the Church: without the world there would be danger of her becoming wrapped up in her own sacredness and uniqueness. The idea of Church and world, not only as distinct, but as existing side by side, each 'on its own', is not without value, especially from a juridical or political, and therefore diplomatic, point of view. But it is insufficient from a spiritual point of view, from that of full Christian existence;

here Church and world are not side by side as in history, but closely entwined. They are not like two crowned sovereigns looking sideways at one another as they sit enthroned on the same dais; they are much more like the Good Samaritan holding in his arms the half-dead man, whom he will not leave because he has been sent to help him; or like a swimmer trying to drag a drowning but struggling man to shore. Bernanos grasped this excellently:

> The Church is something alive, a force at work; but many pious people seem to believe, or pretend to believe, that she is simply a shelter, a place of refuge, a sort of spiritual hotel by the roadside from which they can have the pleasure of watching the passers-by, the chaps outside who are not hotel residents, walking about in the mud.

Anxiety about 'the others', that prompts us to bring faith to bear on certain questions, made Simone Weil frightened of shutting herself up in a society of the redeemed, of baptized persons who would refer to themselves as 'us Christians'. She wrote that 'The Devil says "us" and makes other people say it.' She did not see that, if 'the others' are to be rescued, if the world is to be brought to Christ, we *must* first exist as 'us Christians'. Would to God we lived more that way, that we were more apart from the world and more clearly distinguishable from it, as the Israelites were distinguishable from the Egyptians by the lamb's blood on the lintels of their doors when God passed over! Would to God that we were more sensitive to the meaningful tension between the world and 'us'! When he answered Simone Weil, Father J. M. Perrin brought the two requirements of goodness and completeness, of holiness and all-embracingness, into one:

> To come into the Church is not to cut oneself off from 'the others'. To have a home of one's own can lead to selfish exclusiveness; but it also can enable us to welcome and offer a home to others, helping them to draw nearer

to God 'in the house of the Father here below'. If I may put it so, 'the others' are separated from Christ only by a door that is always open.

A small church in a large world; then, Christianity and other religions; and then, the salvation of 'the others'. . . . At the level of social science there is no solution to the problem. But it is not set at that level; it is set by faith and by two truths of faith, Christ's divinity and the divine founding of the Church. A solution can be looked for only in what faith tells us: that this relatively little thing mediates between two great wholes, Jesus Christ and the world; that they are one for the other, and that the Church's mission is to bring them together and this in two directions, up and down, by representative-ness and by sacrament, as has been explained.

Finally, we will make use of an effective comparison that we owe to our Protestant brothers, that of 'The Church, the *Maquis* of the world'.[1]

A king has been forced to seek refuge in a free country; his kingdom is occupied by invaders. From this far land he pre-pares a counter-invasion in force that shall achieve complete liberation. Meanwhile, in the occupied country, many people have come to terms with the invaders and even work in with them. Most of the people live from day to day, as best they can, waiting for deliverance; they are content occasionally to snatch a few minutes of the secret radio, much as lukewarm Catholics take a breather of Mass and sermon at Christmas and Easter; and that is all. But a certain number of men and women actively reject the enemy's yoke. (In our parable here 'the enemy' of course means the Prince of this world and those malign powers that St Paul speaks of—the worldly forces, both collective and personal, which seek to rule themselves,

---

[1] It is perhaps necessary to explain that during the war of 1939–45 the name *Maquis* was given to the underground liberation movement in France. Literally the word designates the thick undergrowth found in Corsica. *Trans.*

ignoring and even opposing the lordship of Christ.) These resisters, amidst great hardships, strive to live as subjects of the free motherland they hope for and of their true king. They are tireless in their efforts towards liberation; and they are successful in enlisting the help of quite a lot of the half-indifferent, who give support to the resisters from time to time. But the resisters are disinterested men, they work for the liberation and happiness of everyone, without distinction.

When the counter-invasion comes about, deliverance will be due to the resisters *as well as* to the regular military operations. Those people who have had no contacts with them or have despised and opposed them, will then see in the resisters the first-fruits of their recovered freedom: a group representing themselves, who through every trial have kept alive the possibility of a happy future for *all*. This 'all', however, will not mean every single individual, for a number of proved 'collaborators' and traitors will be punished, but 'all' in the sense of the general whole as such.

During those dark days of 1940–5 it used to be said, 'A little Maquis in this big France—what do they think they can do against an enormous giant?' Very much as it is said, 'A small Church in a large world. . . .'

4

Christianity and Other Religions

THIS is not a new problem. The apologists of the second and
third centuries were conscious of it, for they were confronted
by the religions of paganism. But after fifteen hundred years
during which Christendom was more or less a 'closed shop',
the problem took on a fresh acuteness when Christianity was
confronted by heathenism anew. This came about through
the great discoveries, through the colonial and missionary expansion that followed, and eventually, in the eighteenth century, through the new science of religions. All sorts of more
or less reliable information was then brought to the notice of
people in the old Christian lands. The nineteenth century
especially was the age of research into and comparative study
of religions, and there was an inevitable temptation to look
at religions merely from a relative point of view. Do not all
religions claim to originate in a revelation? Have they not
many features in common? Are they not all good if they are
faithfully practised?

The results of this comparative study now do less harm than
they used to do; but the same questions are raised in men's
minds in other ways. People travel. The most strange religious
observances can be seen on the cinema screen. There is a great
mixing of peoples, and the world becomes smaller and smaller.
Furthermore, people are more concerned for what they call
'sincerity' than for truth; minds and their judgements are

unstable; what is 'experienced' is of more interest than what is 'held'. And so our age sees a new questioning of Christianity because of other religions.

'The problem' we have called it, or 'the question'. Really, it is a matter of a whole assemblage of big questions, and we cannot examine all of them here. Moreover, they can be approached in different ways, for people have their own presuppositions and standpoints. Obviously a Moslem, for example, will not put the question in the same way as a Christian; an agnostic, a man without personal faith, or without firm faith, will have his own way of tackling the problem, and that way is clearly not ours.

We are taking the point of view of someone who not only has faith in God but also in Christ. And for such a man there are two ways of approaching our question, apologetically or theologically.

Apologetically, his task is to show others the superiority, and even the divine origin, of Christianity. The matter, then, is stated in terms of comparison; the relative value of each religion under consideration has to be examined. Christianity is shown to be the purest and most lofty, as well as the most universal, having all religious values in their highest form.

On the whole, this was Bergson's way. In *The Two Sources of Morality and Religion* he analyses the religious fact as it is presented to the world, in relation to his own general philosophy of life and evolution. In the world, mankind is the ever-active peak of the evolutionary force (*élan*); amongst men, it is the heroes and saints who ensure progressive improvement. Bergson then estimates the respective worth of different religions, and of the religious ideal (*mystiques*) they show forth, by reference to this line of progress, running into the future; and he proceeds to work out new 'insights'. The highest *mystique*, the best religion, is that of the Christian saints who combine charity and good works with divine contemplation.

But these saints are themselves such only through their loving reference to Jesus Christ, who is the whole secret of their lovingness.

Father Teilhard de Chardin has put forward analogous views within the framework of his great cosmic-Christian[1] synthesis. Natural religions, he says, tied as they are to ideas and myths of the cosmos that are no longer tenable, have been given their death-blow; Christianity, on the contrary, keeps or recovers its youth and prospects in a cosmic evolving setting to which Christ gives meaning and of which he forms the unity, through love.

But here we will put the apologetical point of view on one side. One can believe effectively without having oneself made all the comparisons, just as one can love someone unconditionally without having made a comparative examination of all the other possibilities. Our business here is the dogmatic or theological point of view. The problem is still with us, but in wholly positive terms: starting from what faith tells us about Christianity and its divine character we, as believers, will try to see the relationship of other religions to this Christianity.

THE BEST POSSIBLE RELIGION

Faith's essential affirmation about Christianity is that it is *absolute*. If religion consists in a certain relation of man with God, then the relation of men with God established in and by Jesus Christ is perfect, absolutely. It is not merely perfect *as things are;* there *could not be* any more perfect relationship, or even one that could properly be compared to it. If Jesus Christ is God and man, if mankind and the living God are united in his person, then clearly no religious relationship can equal that, or equal that which it brings about in us through faith. Jesus Christ is *the* religious relationship, he *is* religion.

[1] *Cosmos:* a Greek term signifying the Universe as an ordered whole. *Cosmic:* concerning the whole of all that exists, and not simply mankind.

None other is comparable to the one he institutes, or rather, constitutes; none other can have any value whatever except through him.

Held thus by faith as *absolute*, Christianity could be either exclusive or inclusive with regard to other religions; in other words, it could either refuse them any value whatever or else in some way give them a value.

The Catholic tradition is that Christianity is inclusive. This surely is implied in the way St Paul speaks of the 'mystery of Christ' in the captivity epistles, those to the Ephesians and the Colossians. The mystery of God, realized in Christ and preached by St Paul, comprises the whole of creation, which finds its effective meaning only in Christ. All is for him, and he is for all. We say so at the end of the canon at every Mass: 'Through him and with him and in him are given to you, God the almighty Father, in the unity of the Holy Spirit, all honour and all glory.' A nineteenth-century French philosopher, Ravaisson, put it very penetratingly: 'If Christianity is the meaning of history, then it cannot be absent from any part of history.' And there are those well-known lines of Péguy:

> Every man ended up at the feet of the divine Son;
> Plato's dreams moved towards him . . .
> Zeno's laws moved towards him . . .
> He became the heir of Latin prose . . .

In realizing this, Péguy was in line with an unbroken tradition that runs from today back to the beginning.

In our time, Pope Pius XII took up the theme of preparations for the Gospel, in *Evangelii praecones*.[1] In the twelfth century, there was that striking carving in the chapter-house at Le Puy, showing our Lord on the cross, surrounded by the

[1] In a radio message to the congress at Ernakulam in the following year, 1952, the same Pope said to the Indian Catholics: 'Make sure that people see that everything true and good in other religions finds its deepest meaning and perfect complement in Christ.'

prophets Isaias and Jeremy and Osee, and Philo, the Jewish philosopher who died about A.D. 50; and Philo has a halo round his head, like the others. But it was above all the Fathers of the second, third and fourth centuries who elaborated the idea of a certain presence of the Word in pagan religions: a captive presence, as it were, that had to be freed by the Gospel, a debased and misrepresented presence, that had to be purified by Christ. And indeed everything insufficient or false or idolatrous in heathen religions in a way has got to die so that they may be, in their good elements, taken over by Jesus Christ and in him brought back to the Father. The essential thing is the dogmatic assertion of a certain relation of other religions to the absolute of Christianity, and in the end a restorableness of them to it. Later on we shall see that, as has been hinted in our previous chapter, something analogous must be said of the Church herself, she who is the sacrament of the active presence of Christ in the world.

FAITH AND DISQUIET

We are well aware that such affirmations as these can only be held on to in faith, rather dizzily perhaps. Theologians tell us that faith, while being a firm and unconditional belief in God's word, does not free us from psychological disquiet, the anxiety of a mind that goes on asking itself questions about things all of whose aspects the Christian faith itself has not cleared up. We cannot but ask ourselves from time to time why God allows this. What then is his purpose?

Faith never goes without hope. It believes that it will see, but only at the end. It happens even now, after some very hard trial from which we have not yet fully emerged, but during which we have not failed to 'honour the mystery', that we see with the unshakable certainty of knowledge that *all* has been grace. All has been good, all has been directed towards the end, all has been for the best. Yet all was dark, and seemed to be meaningless. But even before the darkness is dispelled, faith knows that grace is at work, the divine working that drew from St Paul the cry: 'How deep is the mine of God's wisdom, of his knowledge; how inscrutable are his judgements, how undiscoverable his ways! . . . To him be glory throughout all ages, Amen!' (Rom. xi. 33, 36).

5

What is Salvation?

WE are disturbed about the salvation of 'the others'. But what does 'salvation' mean? I have just been going through all the issues of a periodical publication that deals with preaching and catechetics, one that faithfully reflects current ideas and expressions of opinion. In it there is much talk of 'the history of salvation', of 'the mysteries of salvation'—but nowhere in it do I find any explanation of what salvation itself *is*. No doubt the answer to the question is thought to be so elementary that it is taken for granted. But were we to question a number of 'ordinary' Christians on the subject, how many answers should we get that would go beyond a rather mythical and childish idea of it? Are we to be satisfied with 'The wiping out of the stain of original sin and the appeasing of our Father's wrath'?

I do not know whether this matter of salvation has been investigated. Some writings give the impression that the very idea of salvation is questioned nowadays, and that many people reject it. Were it not so, there would be many more waiting to go to confession.

IS IT FINER TO REJECT SALVATION?

It is to be expected that atheism should get rid of the idea of salvation, or at least accept it simply as an achievement of man himself. And consequently the refusal of salvation is

33

sometimes presented as a virtuous act of courage and disinterestedness, worthy of the man 'who knows that he is
swallowed up in nothingness' (M. Thorez). Jacques Maritain
replied to this attitude in *La signification de l'athéisme contem-
porain* (Paris, 1949). But it can be a principle of atheism; it is
at bottom simply a sentimental expression of an aspect of
absolute human autonomy. George Bataille, for example, looks
on salvation as 'the most odious' of bolt-holes, and his inter-
preter, M. Blanchot, writes: 'The principle and purpose of
spiritual life can be found only in the non-existence of salvation and the rejection of all hope.' It is certainly true that
salvation, like hope, implies openness to Another, trust in
Another, the definite handing-over of self and its future to
that Other. Jacques Rivière felt this when he wrote to Claudel
in 1913: 'Not to be a Christian means that one finds reason
enough in this life alone. For me, this sufficient reason lies in
knowledge of myself. . . . How far I am from God! I feel myself
to be wholly given up by him and able to do without him.'

There is something noble about these declarations, they
appeal to something good in the depths of the human heart;
and for that reason they can make us realize, in the very
measure that we reject them, what salvation means for us:
they express in reverse things that we hold in their fullness.
And so they remind us of what salvation involves. Hope for
afterwards. After what? After things that can be seen, things
that are experienced by our senses and measured by our
instruments. Then, the insufficiency of this life and our own
insufficiency for ourselves. And lastly, trust in Another—a
Saviour, in fact—who opens the way to what lies beyond
ourselves and this present life.

But, no doubt because we have referred to men of letters
who are themselves deeply disturbed, many Christians would
refuse to recognize the salvation they look for in affirmations
that are simply the contrary of the writers' negations. Many

people nowadays are ill at ease before any presentation of salvation that strikes them as one-sided, and therefore inadequate. 'To save souls' is a fine expression, but they are worried at its incompleteness—what about bodies? Or the individualism of 'I have only one soul, and I want to save it'. Today, in one form or another, we are always meeting this obsession with a total, cosmic salvation, with the solidarity *of all* in it. 'We must reach God in a body, together. We must come before him together. It will not do for some of us to find God without the others.' So wrote Péguy.

WE ARE BEGINNING TO TAKE SIN SERIOUSLY

Whether it be concern for 'the whole' and for history, or concern for the individual person, it is always a matter of man and of the world. These two tendencies (which are found carried to their extremes in the opposed attitudes of Marxism and of 'man in revolt')[1] anyway have this in common for our purpose—that they look only at the fulfilment of man and his world, and have no notion whatever of the idea of being saved from any danger, from any divine wrath, from any hell or damnation.

Here we have to take notice of another aspect of the Christian idea of salvation: it involves the possibility of falling into a pit and being lost there. That seems unbelievable to modern rationalism—that a man, that the world, can fall short of their destiny. Are they not their own destiny? Is it not in their own hands? Fundamentally, the great rationalist debate is not over. There is always the question of whether man stands alone, absolutely self-governing, or whether he has a relationship, a 'dialogue', with God, his Creator, and is open to the advances of divine love. At all events, people are beginning again to take the idea of deadly sin more seriously (it has

[1] Camus accused Marxism of reducing men to being merely material for history, whereas every one of them has a unique destiny.

never been altogether forgotten), and with it the idea of Hell: the condition of despair, from which there is no way out or end, of a man who has failed his destiny, and who knows it. Properly understood, this mystery of Hell itself enables us to understand many other things. It gives their depth to a number of Christian affirmations, and in the first place to that of everlasting salvation, of which Hell is the correlative. *Salvation can be lost.*

Their eyes enthusiastically fixed on the world, men today are led to forget one of salvation's two aspects. In the same way and for the same reason, they are apt to do the same thing where freedom is concerned. There is a classical but still very instructive distinction made between 'freedom *from*' and 'freedom *to*'; on one side, liberation, release, disengagement; on the other, self-giving, service, engagement. So with salvation. It can be looked at with reference to a danger, to a possibility of losing all, including life itself; we can be saved from a cruel, tyrannous, death-dealing enemy. And it can also be looked at with reference to the life, the happiness, the fullness to which this deliverance restores us, the possibility of which our saviour, our rescuer, opens to us.

THE DOUBLE ASPECT OF SALVATION

Earlier Christians were keenly conscious of the first of these aspects of salvation. They, and especially the men of the middle ages, emphasized the painfulness and difficulty of the act that sets us free, and the necessity for expiation and atonement. For they believed in sin, they believed in the Devil and in Hell. Most important of all, they believed in God, by reference to whom alone can the Christian idea of sin and its wickedness be understood. When the Fathers of the Church compared our situation to that of a shipwrecked man whose only hope of safety is a floating piece of wood—the wood of the Cross—they were not denying the value of the world; but they knew the gloriousness of God, and were testifying to a keen consciousness of the frightful calamity that sin brings on us and of the need for help from God himself. Even when the time comes, on the other side of the 'sea of glass, tinged with fire', for us to sing the Song of Moses and the Song of the Lamb—as the Apocalypse (xv. 2–3) shows God's chosen ones doing—the lines of an English poet will remain true:

> But none of the ransomed ever knew
> How deep were the waters crossed.

People today look at the maximum outcome of salvation, its positive results and boons. If, in relation to the world, salvation can mean either 'to be saved from this world' or 'that this world is saved', they are resolutely for the second meaning. In 1946 *La Vie spirituelle* conducted an inquiry on the subject of holiness, and in it could be found many an expression of this general attitude. What it came to was that many people, innocently enough, professed to revere the holiness of the second great commandment, without saying much about the holiness of the first, which turns our eyes Godward.

For a long time—perhaps for near enough three hundred years—the most tragic and pernicious thing about Christianity's situation in the modern world has doubtless been this rift between the first and the second great commandment, between theology and anthropology—it is clean contrary to the Gospel and to the whole Bible. There are some people who, provided Vespers be sung to the correct plainsong modes, are hardly disturbed by human misfortune; there are others— much more numerous—who are not concerned with praising God provided men succeed in their undertakings. We reject this false 'Either . . . or' absolutely; it is a most mischievous equivocation. Where salvation is concerned, we equally refuse either to give preference to its aspect of deliverance from peril, damnation, with the time of painful redemption that goes with it, or to separate its positive aspect of glorious fulfilment from its hard conditions and from the moment of rescue that is its first phase.

The Bible, and the Tradition within which the Church has lived it, present the fact of salvation *both* as deliverance or rescue and as fulfilment.

'IT IS GOD'S GLORY THAT MAN LIVES'

The Old Testament prophets never tire of presenting the messianic age, the object of Israel's hope, as bringing a salvation which shall not only be deliverance, but fruitfulness, peace and abundance of good things.[1] It is true that their language is hyberbolical and pictorial, but it expresses matters that cannot just be reduced to oriental poetry. Besides, what does Jesus say and do when he presents himself as the one who is to fulfil these promises? After reading the messianic announcement in Isaias lxi. 1–2, he shuts the book and says, 'The scripture which I have read in your hearing is today fulfilled' (Luke iv. 21); he defines his mission as 'to search out and to save what was lost' (*ib.* xix. 10). What he does is the best commentary on what he says: he heals the sick, restores the dead to life, makes the cripple whole, gives back dignity and self-respect to the oppressed and humiliated and the downtrodden generally. That is the meaning of the many narratives of healing that are read in the gospels at Mass on the Sundays after Pentecost.

What do Christ's apostles say, when they proclaim him as Saviour after Pentecost? What but that he saves by the Cross, and that all salvation involves conversion and detachment? But they also say that there is a salvation of achievement for the world, a promise of fullness of life beyond itself and its

[1] Rabbi A. Neher insists on the inclusion of the covenant with Noe, having in view the natural order (Gen. viii. 15–22), in the covenant of grace. A. Neher: *Moses* (Longmans, England and Harper, U.S.A., 1959.)

present wretched state. St Peter speaks of 'the time when all is restored anew' (Acts iii. 21), and St Paul writes of bringing *all things* under Christ as head, of reconciling *all things* to him (Eph. i. 10, 23; Col. i. 20).

When Christ's friends and followers put their testimony into writing in the four gospels, to what use do they show their Master, and ours, putting the verb 'to save'?[1] The gospels set out no theory of the Redemption, but give a number of very concrete applications of the word 'save'. It often appears in accounts of healing, where continued life is ensured by circumventing things that are harmful to it, things which are also opposed to God and his purpose. Sometimes 'salvation' has reference to the expected terrible ending of things, and so to being saved from God's anger and entering into the Kingdom, there to inherit everlasting life. Then, in St Luke, these ideas are taken in a theological and deeply moral sense: salvation is a deliverance, above all deliverance from sin and its disastrous consequences. This is found especially in those famous canticles that accompany the birth of Jesus, the *Magnificat*, the *Benedictus* and Simeon's *Nunc dimittis*, lovely hymns that are sung solemnly at Vespers, Lauds and Complin.

From the Fathers, we will quote only one sentence, from St Irenaeus, who is the oldest of them, perhaps the most unalloyedly Christian, and a bond of union between West and East; in about the year 180 he wrote: 'It is God's glory that man lives!' The liturgy, which is the sacred shrine of the Church's tradition, expresses the same thing, with a confidence equalled only by its carefulness, at the fine beginning of Matins for the dead: 'Come, let us worship the King for whom all things live.' But it is simply an echo of the Bible: cf. Wisdom xi. 24–27.

[1] For numerous references to the scriptural use and meanings of the words *soteria*, salvation, and *sozein*, to save, see W. Barclay, *A New Testament Wordbook* (Harper, U.S.A., 1957 and London, 1959), pp. 114–21 [Trans.]

BEYOND SELF, BEYOND DEATH

What, then, does 'to be saved' mean? From what must we be saved?

It would take many pages to detail all the particulars of the Christian answer, showing their relationship and how they make a great whole. But Étienne Borne gave its essential elements when he wrote:

> First of all Christianity throws into relief those tyrannies under which we labour, tyrannies that are humanly invincible, for their names are death, aloneness, sin. But the same Christianity (and this, precisely, is the Good News) reveals to us that the free God is a freeing God, that he destroys the deceptive fatality of those tyrannies and calls us to eternity, to fellowship, to holiness.

The living hope for which every Christian fights and strives to attain his Easter comprises the following four points.

(1) To have a destiny *beyond.* Beyond what? Beyond my own possibilities and those of humankind and the world. For I am wickedly treated, and find myself powerless to obtain real justice, unfortunate, and powerless to repair my fortunes, a sinner, and powerless to cleanse myself. . . . All the potions in the world cannot prevent me from growing old, wearing out and dying, for all that I want to live, my powers untouched by time's hand. . . . That is the state we are in, and it is just about what the Fathers and spiritual writers describe as 'distress' (*miseria*), or 'frustration', as St Paul puts it (Rom. viii. 20); it produces a feeling of uneasiness in us, or what may be called, following Kierkegaard, 'dread'. This is because we are continually reaching 'the limit', with a breath left to go beyond it—but only a fitful, fruitless gasp.

Again, beyond what? Beyond myself. For if I am a person, something unique, a thing in itself and for itself, then I form part of the very structure of the world: of the human world, as a link in the chain of generations, as heir to the culture of the ages, and through those strong social bonds thanks to which in large measure I am what I am; but not of the human world only—of the so-called material world as well.

Fundamentally, the universe is one whole. It is precisely that for the Bible; the Greeks called it Cosmos; the Fathers and the Christian middle ages spoke of man as the microcosm, the epitome that sums up and completes the vast world with which we have community of material substance and of general destiny. For them, the world, material or simply living, attained personal consciousness in man; and man, being a person in himself, remained in solidarity with the world, and also became as it were responsible for it from the point of view of its higher destiny. It is on this very ground and in this way that we, immortal souls animating a body taken from the dust of this earth, are the first-fruits of the world. My destiny is not that of an isolated soul; taken integrally, it is that of the world of which I am part, which acts on me and on which I act.

Yet again, beyond what? Beyond death—the last and chief reason for our distress—and so beyond this present life. We have reached *the* point. The salvation that Christ brings is above all a saving from death and therefore from nothingness. Through faith I know that I shall live, I myself and all myself, with my body, for ever. Above everything else, faith is for me the boundless trust I put in Christ that he will govern my life, for he has promised that I shall live beyond death, a life that is without end.

(2) Salvation depends essentially on someone else, for it consists in a going beyond myself and my own possibilities and my present life. It is not in man's power, or the world's: it is in the Lord's power. Jesus, as true God and true man, is able to join God's power to man's insufficiency; and it is he who, as priest, has offered for the whole world the sacrifice that is the foundation-stone of the restoring of fellowship with God. It is

Jesus who, as King of the ages, imparts to men, and through them to the world, the fruits of that restored fellowship; and it is precisely these in their totality that constitute salvation as consummation and fulfilment.

(3) It follows from all this that salvation gives a meaning to our present life in terms of this hope for the future, a 'beyond', and of Jesus Christ who revealed it and brings it to pass; and it also prompts us to strive to anticipate in the world itself (in so far as we can influence it) something which, by linking the world with Christ, is a foretaste of the destiny he offers it. For, as we stagger to the limit of our efforts, an inspiration impels us to try to go farther, and that inspiration comes through the faith and love of the sons of God (cf. Rom. viii. 19–27). It is not just mankind in general, but very precisely *they* who are the first-fruits of a saved world. The meaning that salvation gives to our life is such that it secures the full meaning, not only to life here where we are birds of passage, but also hereafter, where we are called to live for ever. To lose salvation is to lose life's meaning. We shall see later on that Hell is essentially the culmination of a situation in which the distress that afflicts us is finally made permanent.

(4) Freedom from 'frustration'. Life's meaning is bound up with a right relationship between us creatures and God our creator. At the deepest level, this relationship consists in so conducting ourselves that we allow God to be really God in us, shining in and through us, fulfilling his will in and through us. To hinder God being God in us, for us and, through us, for all that depends on us, is to sin. And the most fundamental condition for salvation is that sin should be overcome and cast aside.

Our sins: we are not exactly obsessed by them! Yet. . . . In A. J. Cronin's *The Keys of the Kingdom*, the unbelieving doctor Willie Tulloch, as a boy, provoked a fight with a schoolfellow by saying mockingly that Catholics could get their sins forgiven by paying sixpence; but as he lay dying years later he murmured, 'I would give more than sixpence to get my sins forgiven.' It has been said that Buddhism would save man from suffering, but that Christianity would save him from sin: it is indeed a redemption. But from the outset of our inquiry we have disclaimed any intention of entering here on a theology of the Redemption. Nevertheless that is where Jesus Christ, our Saviour, is at work from the very first.

6

Heaven, Salvation and World History

ONE of the most penetrating things ever said about Heaven is Newman's remark that were a wicked man to go there he would not know that he was in Heaven.

That saying might provoke an objection: 'But there would be the angels, with their rustling wings and robes, the pink clouds and the soft blue of the atmosphere, and the flowers, and the sound of singing. . . . And he would see God, and our Lady and the saints. . . .' No; a wicked man would not see God; to do that, one must be clean of heart (Matt. v. 8).

To put it another way, the kingdom of God is first of all within us.[1] No one knows God unless he has first been known by God, known with that merciful knowledge which does not *presuppose* that we are conformed to him but which *makes* us so. Heaven is not to be thought of at once as an external order of nice things, a sort of pleasure fair, where the admission-ticket gives us the run of every attraction.[2] Just as with Hell and Purgatory, so with Heaven; we must now put away our stupidly superficial this-worldly imaginings, and try to understand things in the spiritual context of Salvation and the

[1] When it was said to the holy Russian monk Seraphim of Sarov (d. 1833) that his body appeared luminous, he replied, 'That is not surprising, for the kingdom of God is within us.'

[2] Let us get rid of everything of this sort: 'As the end of their journey, the elect do not aim at the peaks of the Andes or the Himalayas, but at a walk in the Milky Way' (J. Souben, *Nouvelle théologie dogmatique*, 1906, p. 73). Who are we taken for?

Covenant, in a way that shall not be too unworthy of God or of ourselves, or of the world, for Heaven is not the negation of the world but its pattern, the pattern first lost, and then restored by grace.

Heaven is really *a saving* wherein that which all earthly history strives after is received as a gift from above. Here we are looking at things in this light particularly, and not under the obviously chief aspect of the vision of God's essence, which involves quite another chapter in theology. The general purpose of this little book is to direct the mind along a different line, but one that is no less authentic and deserving of attention.

THE GREAT AIMS OF HUMAN HISTORY

Human history strives after two things. First, to bring back integrity to man, damaged as he is by so many evils and painful limitations; to enable him to progress in the way he longs to and cannot, for he feels within himself an urge to go beyond the limit he is always reaching, where he is made miserable by his inability to attain the end towards which he is impelled. This longing is, in a last analysis, to conquer death and decay and disease and all that leads to death. And, too, to overcome all the hindrances that hurt and thwart us, and cut us off from and put us at enmity with things and other men, we who are made to love and be loved, made for harmony, unitedness, peace and fellowship. When we reflect on the events of history, on what men are ever seeking, we see that, more or less closely, in one way or another, it is always a matter of these two things: to vanquish what is limiting and hurtful—infirmity, sickness, ignorance, triviality of life, social tyranny, fear of insecurity, and at the end death; and to overcome separations and divisions.

It is very true that history is also full of violence and injustice, which make things worse instead of better. Man is like that: he seeks happiness by destroying himself, seeks peace through war, prosperity through theft. But it is still happiness and peace and prosperity that he is seeking. He simply is mistaken about the way to get them.

But not altogether. There is also a certain inevitability about it; or better, man obeys a certain pattern or law of that earthly history in which he is the chief actor. The law of this history is not simply endeavour, the straightforward use of energy that meets plenty of inertia but not active opposition or contradiction.

History is not only effort, it is also conflict. It goes forward through conflict and thanks to it. It has a 'two-way' structure, it works through tension. It may be said, it must be said, that it is dialectical.[1] That is why evil and suffering are inherent in it. It seeks to get rid of them, but is able to do so only by arousing and carrying on conflicts, and in so doing it takes on itself the evil it wants to destroy. The goal of history is not just a coming to maturity, it is a *victory*.

(Notice in passing that God himself entered into human history *up to that very point*. What we call the Redemption, what St Paul calls the wisdom of the Cross, is precisely that!)

It will be thus, so long as the goal is not reached, that is, so long as things do not become wholly manifest and clear *from within* themselves, transparent, as it were. Without that, things remain superficial to one another, and can seek to be at one only subject to a separateness that inevitably involves elements of externality, and therefore of misunderstanding and opposition. In this world the quest for inwardness itself starts from outwardness. Until they are surmounted, external things are, not only a condition, but one of the means in the battle to defeat them. Our gains in this life are made by going from outside to inside. We overcome bodily weakness by eating

---

[1] *Dialectical:* proceeding from a conflict of contradictions that produces a 'higher' synthesis. [*Trans.*]

food; we overcome sickness by taking medicine; we overcome ignorance by receiving knowledge from the world, through experience and teaching, through eyes and ears; and we go towards sight of God through the outward things of faith. Friendship and love grow from intercourse between persons; but if they are to be joined together, those persons must first meet, face to face or side by side: inwardness is brought about by outwardness—but outwardness makes us suffer all the same.

Unitedness, then, is brought about, perfection and fulfilment acquired, through receiving from outside; and it is this which, in the end, accounts for the good that we get from external compulsion in our quest for inwardness and fullness of life— from education, social life, our work, law (which has necessarily to be enforced). Even in that most intimate matter, communion with God, there must be external means to its achievement and growth, for all that its deepest manifestation seeks to go farther and leave them behind. There is mediation by Christ and by the Church, by religious instruction and by the sacraments; on Sinai, the Covenant was made on the basis of the Law, and the Law, fulfilled in the Gospel, is holy. I can meet with God only by fulfilling many requirements imposed on me from outside. Every religious man or woman suffers in consequence; he wants God *himself* to be wholly within him, and God is still so far away, even though he is so close.

But the problem goes far beyond the religious sphere. We all suffer from these outward things which necessarily coerce us:

Nature and mind. Mind has the primacy, but nature crushes it. It is rather like spirit and flesh: sometimes spirit is 'on the spot' and flesh is weak; sometimes spirit is weak and flesh smothers it.

Man and woman, face to face. Often, alas! they baffle each other, are like strangers to one another.

We are all caught up in social life; but each person is interested only in his own troubles, and ultimately in himself, and cannot enter into those of others. In such conditions 'Other people are hell'.

Germans and French, Africans and Europeans, each with their own language, culture and aspirations: that produces a situation pregnant with mutual recriminations and eventually bloody collisions.

Need we go on with the list?

That outwardness which separates things from the meaning of things, events from the meaning of events, so that we are unable to understand them and so find them hard to endure. But the meaning of expressions of the spirit, that is partly elusive too and we do not understand them. This is true even of the holy Scriptures, which are not fully self-explanatory, so that there has to be interpretation, a tradition, a teaching authority, the Church.

The social and the personal. Power does not coincide with understanding, still less with love and holiness—and how often they suffer in consequence!

'THAT GOD MAY BE ALL IN ALL'

When the Kingdom comes, it will confirm and take over all man's *good* strivings to overcome the wretchedness and hindrances from which he suffers, for, whether consciously or not, those strivings work for God's purposes.[1] Once again, Heaven is a 'saving'; Jesus came 'to search out and to save *what was lost*' (Luke xix. 10). Were it not for the taking over and confirming of our good strivings, *they* at least would be lost, and Heaven would not be that just reward of which the Gospel speaks; but in spite of this Heaven is over and above all a gift, a grace, and one infinitely surpassing our 'merits'

[1] See Y. Congar, *Lay People in the Church* (London and Westminster, Md., 1957), pp. 77ff.; cf. below p. 166.

(which themselves are a fruit of God's gifts) and the success of all the efforts ever made to triumph over afflictions and obstacles. God will freely give us the fullness of what he has bestowed on us and asked us to begin.

We will give an outline of what this plenitude means. St Paul has summed it up in seven words, themselves of surpassing content and depth: 'that God may be all in all' (1 Cor. xv. 28). All we wish to do here is to comment on these words, aided by a few reflections from the Fathers of the Church.

> To the Lord belongs the heaven of heavens,
> the earth he gives to the children of men.

That verse of Psalm 113 is a good summary of the first account of creation in the book of Genesis. It seems that when God had made the universe or at least the earth, he gave it to man to rule and subdue, whilst he himself rested in Heaven on the seventh day (Gen. i. 28; ii. 2–3). If we consider this universe, it would appear that, before it was, there was God; after the universe was, and above it, there still was God: but between the two there was the earth, given to men and having the quality of a thing finished and well made. That is about how things look to us, and we can accommodate ourselves to them very well. Many people's religion corresponds closely enough to this pattern, in which God is recognized as having created at the beginning and in which he is expected at the end when, on leaving this world, men will find themselves in his presence —steps can be taken to ensure that the meeting shall not be too uncomfortable nor the questions too searching. . . . But *this* world is left to us, to be lorded over and enjoyed: *God is absent from it.* That is why so many men, who do not deny God's existence, are nevertheless atheists in practice, in the sense that they use the earth as if he were not there.

We can give this meaning (which is not his) to Origen's remark that we do not see the beginning and end of things, but only what is in between. The middle is enough for us: we build our life on it, and so that life becomes this-worldly, profane, 'not sacred'.

Now there is one aspect of things that faith does not change, and that is the things themselves, in their physical nature. A mile is a mile, an apple is an apple, a toothache is a toothache, with faith or without it. Nature knows nothing of holiness; a typhoon will bring down a church as soon as a barracks or a school. But there is another aspect that faith does affect and change, and that is the *use* we make of things, the *meaning* that we give to them, to things that happen, to human encounters. The Christ of the Gospel and of the Church is not yet the victorious King, but he is even now the Master of living; and he teaches us to see things *as having their beginning and end present in them*, and to use them accordingly. He teaches us not to look for the light that explains things in the things themselves, in the 'middle' (that is the business of science and technology); but to look for that too in their beginning and their end, that is, beyond themselves. That means, to look for it in the Gospel, in so far as the Gospel touches life on earth; to look for it in the reign of Jesus Christ and God, in so far as that reign is established on earth and in temporal matters.

The whole earthly order of the Body of Christ, the Church, has that in view: there is the call for faith, for suffering patiently, for spiritual warfare, for love. We have to rid ourselves of a selfish habit, of a purely wordly habit, by which man seeks only 'that which is his', his own interests; instead, we have to learn to see the world as *God's* world, as a world whose beginning is the Father's heart and hands, its end his arms and his love: not as *man's* world, one meant solely for *self*. Only faith can do this, faith as the source of a conversion that is as demanding as it is thorough. Only the Cross can do this, for we never give up our comforts and our selfishness unless we are forced. Only love can do this: because it is love that gives back their meaning to things by making us see God in them, as Dostoevsky sets out so finely, especially through the mouth of Father Zossima in *The Brothers Karamazov* (cf below, pp. 60–61).

HEAVEN, GOD'S HOUR

Faith, the Cross and love, the three foundations of Christian life, mark the beginnings in this world of a shadowy reign of God, which will achieve the glory of complete victory in his Kingdom. They begin to make his will to be done on earth *as it is in Heaven*—but it is only a beginning. For those who have longed and worked for his day, God's hour will come— and that will be Heaven.

God will be all in all. He is that already, since without him nothing can exist; but the glory is wanting, because he is not acknowledged, he is not longed for, loved and praised, as being the beginning and end of everything. In this world, during the course of earthly history, Heaven is being prepared in the hearts of the faithful. but nebulously, fragmentarily, pre-cariously. But to a great extent people behave as if the 'middle' of things were enough for them, as if things could continue to exist without their Beginning and could have their truth inde-pendently of reference to their End. Save for the faithful, who restore it to them as best they can, the meaning of things remains external to the things, and difficult to discern; very often it is purely and simply ignored, left undeciphered and unknown.

But in Heaven it becomes *plain* that God is the beginning and the end. Henceforward it is quite clear, not through a toilsome and uncertain proceeding from outside to inside, but through the shining manifestation of the Source himself, who is more inward to things than things are to themselves. By the strength of this light things become transparent. They not only have meaning; they reveal and tell, they shout their meaning, their ultimate meaning, their meaning in relation to the absolute Beginning and End. It is not only seen that God is their beginning and end; it is seen *in what manner* he is that, has been that, and will be that for ever.

It sometimes happens, after an event that closes a chapter of life for us, that we look back over all that has gone before; for instance, at the death of a great friend, when we recall all that we did together, or at the moment of some big change in our life, or—a more commonplace example—when we are going away and make a last effort to clear things up. We look back over a past that has had its shadows, its troubles, its trying times, and we say to ourself, 'Ah well! I have done what I could, and on the whole it has all been pretty good.' So Josue, who had fought some hard campaigns and come through many dangers, recognized on his death-bed that God had ordered all things well, and he called on others to recognize it too: 'The time has come when I must go the way all mortal things go at last; and I would have you cherish this message deep in your hearts. Of all the promises the Lord made you, not one has missed fulfilment' (Joshua xxiii. 14).

Something like that will happen in Heaven, both as regards world history and our own personal lives. The world's history is so very often obscure, up and down and disconcerting, but at its end we shall understand the meaning of things from their inward depth, which is God. We shall see that it was God in everything; and we shall also see how he was in everything according to what he is, *Himself*, that is, Love and Justice, 'All our questionings and agonies and resentments have one and the same origin, namely, that for us God is not God. . . . Heaven will be the seeing of how God is God' (L. Evely).

For that very reason Heaven is also thanksgiving. It will even be simply that: the recognition of the fact that everything is from God, and that everything which is from him is good, holy, true and life-giving; the understanding of a history, ended at last, which while we were living it seemed hardly more than a tangle of many-coloured threads, like a tapestry in the making; the heartfelt assent to God's will and purposes. St Augustine says that the whole business of Heaven will be the expression of this assent in praise: 'We shall say Alleluia because we shall say Amen!';[1] and St Thomas Aquinas writes that in Heaven all worship is *gratiarum actio et vox laudis*, 'thanksgiving and songs of praise'.

God all in all. He is that from everlasting; but St Paul puts it in the future. It is in that that his Kingdom will consist. In this world it is *we* who are at work, or at least we claim to be. We do *our* work, pursue *our* undertakings, look after *our* interests. The earth is a human earth, not just in the interesting and affectionate sense given to that phrase by Saint-Exupéry, but in the man-centred sense of a world left in a way to man and his enterprises and control.

God's Sabbath will come, the everlasting Sunday; a *Lord's* day on a new earth that will have become wholly *the Lord's* earth. We shall cease from works that are only ours and which we attribute to ourselves; instead, we shall see and know that it is *God* who is the author of all good, and we shall at last let him be God in all his fullness, the sovereign doer. The Fathers wrote superbly on this subject; here is a passage from St Augustine, at the end of his *City of God* (bk. xxii, c. 30):

> For we ourselves shall be the seventh day, when we shall be replenished to overflowing with his blessing and holiness. Freed from toil, we shall see that he is God, which we ourselves wanted to be when we fell away from him, listening to the promise of the Seducer, 'You yourselves will be like gods' (Gen. iii. 5). Restored by him, perfected by a greater

[1] *Sermo* 162, 29 (P.L., 39, 1633). Augustine has some fascinating passages on Alleluia as the heavenly song: *Enarr. in Ps.* 148, 1 (37, 1938); *Sermo* 243, 8 (38, 1147); 252, 9 (1176–7), with the phrase *actio quietis* = Alleluia; 255, 1, 5 (1186, 1188); 256 (1190ff.).

grace, we shall rest for ever, seeing that he is God, God who will replenish us when he is all in all. For when we understand that they are more his than ours, then our good works are put to our credit that we may gain the Sabbath without end. If we attribute them to ourselves, they are but the work of slaves, and it is said of the Sabbath that you shall do no servile work thereon. And the prophet Ezechiel says:'I gave them also my sabbaths, to be a sign between me and them, and that they might know that it is *I, the Lord*, who sanctifies them' (Ezech. xx. 12). But we shall recognize this perfectly only when we are perfectly and happily at rest and see perfectly that *he is* God.

May we quote Péguy after that? The poetry of his hymn to night is not unworthy of Augustine's theology. He makes God say:

For man, in his toil, glorifies me only through his toil.
And in sleep it is I who glorify myself through man's
    forsaking . . .
Gentle, vast, lovely night, holiest perhaps of all my
    daughters,
Night of the enfolding robe, the star-girt robe—
You bring back to me the world's great silence
Before man's reign therein;
You foretell the great silence that will be
When that reign ends, when I shall have again
Taken up my sceptre.

THE FINAL RESTORATION AND RECONCILIATION

God will be all in all. One would not dare to say that if St Paul had not written it first; he having done so, it is for us to take it very seriously, for Paul was a Jew turned Christian and he knew the full implications of the oneness of God. He is the one God, there is not any other, and he cannot be confused with any other; but he is also *truly God*, he acts as such, and his glory is in being left to be God, in being recognized as truly God, working supremely in all things.

That means that he, the One, will bring all light to me—
he will *be* my light; he will bring me peace and happiness—
he will *be* my peace and happiness. And so for everything. And
for everybody.

God himself will use his power to consummate the creation
he started on its way (leaving it the danger of hurting itself);
he will finish the sketch on which at present he leaves us to
work as best we can: we see clearly from these truths that the
finally restored creation of which St Peter speaks, following
Jesus himself (Acts iii. 21; Matt. xix. 28), will have that
integrity that creation strives for. Heaven is untouched by all
the ignorance, the disease, the weakness, the degradation,
the poverty that we suffer from; it is beyond death, which will
be the last thing to be destroyed (1 Cor. xv. 26). Things, life
and ourselves will no longer exist in separation from their
meaning; the inward signification of all will shine before the
eyes of all. This return of 'transparency' to created beings will
deliver them from that frustration to which, as St Paul says
(Rom. viii. 20) they are now condemned, and they will be
free.

This world is full of compulsions and constraints because it
can reach its inwardness only from outside, and to do that it
has need of other things and other men; we remain external
to these, and we oppose and conflict with them. But when
everything is given from within and when each being simply
shows what he is, this inwardness and 'transparency' give
freedom. St Paul makes this freedom the mark of 'the revelation of the sons of God' for which 'creation is full of expectancy'
(Rom. viii. 19ff.). So long as action does not coincide spon-
taneously with its truth, an external law is necessary; but
action whose truth springs from within has recovered spon-
taneity and freedom.

The one God being all *in all*, a principle of perfect fellowship will be at work throughout the new creation. The English

word 'atonement', meaning both expiation (redemption) and reconciliation, is sometimes written in its three elements, at-one-ment', making one, return to oneness, recovery of fellowship. From the Lord's Passover and from God-all-in-all will be born a world wholly 'at-oned', wholly beyond the oppositions and failures to communicate and to combine that afflict us in this present life, as between 'Greek and barbarian' (native and foreigner), 'slave and freeman' (wage-earner and employer), 'man and woman'.[1]

It is not for nothing that all the comparisons our Saviour makes when speaking of the Kingdom or of Heaven express a single-minded gathering of many people together, with a background of accomplishment and rejoicing: a city, a house, a wedding-feast, a kingdom are all images that express something in which individuals are present and at the same time form a whole together. The old division of person and totality, which so often leads to opposition between them, must disappear.

We know, for we have sometimes had the happy experience, that this opposition breaks down when love is truly present. One would suppose that when a man gives himself, he loses himself; but it is not so. He finds himself. He fulfils a need of human nature, deep below the superficial calls of selfishness, the need for fellowship with other people, and even with all living creatures and with the things that we call inanimate as well. Our true personality is not the one that asserts itself, noisily and tiresomely and sometimes at the expense of others: no, it is the one that loves and gives. This is the only one that will continue in Heaven, for 'we shall never have finished with

---

[1] Cf. Gal. iii. 26–28; Rom. x. 12. In the so-called 'Second' Letter of Clement to the Corinthians (xii. 2) there is a passage, having a flavour of a sect hostile to marriage, but significant for our purpose: 'When someone asked the Lord when his kingdom would come, he answered: "When two (things) make one, when outside is like inside, when in the meeting of man with woman there will no longer be either man or woman".'

charity' (1 Cor. xiii. 8). And many people who on earth were distinguished but loveless, 'great' victors, 'great stars' of all kinds, will be brought down to almost nothing; while others, 'little men', people crushed by life, will be seen to be truly great and fine.

Because Heaven will be the revelation of love—love that really deserves the name—it will bring about at the same time the fullest development both of personality and of community. There my happiness will be more than ever mine, God will be more than ever my God; yet no one will say 'my God', 'my happiness'; it will be 'our God', 'our happiness'; and the same with all the good things with which we shall be filled, together, by the one Source of all things.[1]

We speak of 'the communion of saints' and this grand expression must be given its full force, the strongest meaning that the word 'communion', fellowship, can have, in a social sense as well as in theology. It is something other than an external order produced by an authority that brings dispersed forces together in order to obtain a result in common. In communion in its pure state there is no outwardness, there is no coercive authority, there is not necessarily even co-operation for a given end: but there is give-and-take, 'transparency', being present to one other and giving to one another. Giving of what? Of all that one has, but more still: giving of self, giving of persons themselves to other persons, each being seen for what he is, each being accepted for what he is. The supreme example is the communion of the Three Divine Persons. We are far away from complete fellowship here on earth; but Heaven will be a perfected communion of saints, a perfected fellowship of persons. The thought of this great hope reminds us of certain

---

[1] Cf. St Augustine: 'May we delight in whatever can be brought with us to that kingdom where no one says "my Father", but all say to the one God, "our Father"; and not "my mother", but all to that Jerusalem, "our mother"; and not "my brother", but all say of each, "our brother" ' (*De sermone Dni. in monte*, 1, 41).

words from Russia, in which can be found the inspiration, through Dostoevsky, of the New Testament itself:

'When the gospels say that in the kingdom of God there are neither Jews nor Gentiles, do they just mean that all are equal in the sight of God? I don't believe it means only that—that was known already—it was known to the Greek philosophers and the Roman moralists and the Hebrew prophets. What the gospels tell us is that in this new way of life and of communion, which is born of the heart and which is called the Kingdom of God, there are no nations but only persons.

'Now you said that facts don't mean anything by themselves—not until a meaning is put into them. Well—the meaning you have to put into the facts to make them relevant to human beings is just that: it's Christianity, it's the mystery of personality.[1]

This perfect communion, however, is not a fusion. Each person remains himself and hears his own name. When we echo St Paul and say 'God all in all' we are not affirming any ridiculous pantheism. God is God, and each man is himself. God has put us outside himself: not, of course, that there could be any outside whatever to God, but in the sense that has made us distinct, having our own being, which is not God's being; we are persons who for ever are able to say 'I'. When St Clare of Assisi was dying, she exclaimed, 'O God, thank you for creating me.' Yes, I for ever shall be a unique spark, irreplaceable, having my own name, in a Home that includes them all without absorbing them. To this aspect of the final state of the world St Maximus the Confessor applied the symbol of the Burning Bush (Exod. iii. 2–6): 'This fire, unutterable, tremendous, hidden in the essence of things as in a bush.' It is the divine energy, the energy of the God who creates without withholding their own being from things, but giving it to

[1] B. Pasternak, *Doctor Zhivago* tr. by Max Hayward and Manya Harari (Harvill, England and Pantheon, U.S.A., 1958), p. 117.

them: 'I am He who is'; 'Behold, I make all things new' (*ib.* iii. 14; Apoc. xxi. 5).

Heaven is this newness of mankind, when men are at last fully in His image and in the image of the risen Lord.

HEAVEN IS WHERE GOD IS FULLY GOD

To see God! Heaven will be to see God. Yes, and how more than satisfying this vision will be! It will be deifying; for we shall see, not an idea of God, but God himself, making himself known and enjoyed directly and substantially by his immediate, perfect, active Presence.

In accordance with our general purpose, we have in these pages discussed Heaven in its aspect as salvation of the world, the fulfilment of creation in God's kingdom and through his reign. Heaven is where God reigns wholly, where he is fully God, where he is fully active and fully acknowledged as the beginning and end of all things. There we shall see that God is God, and how he is God, and how he has been God throughout the twofold history of the world and of grace; we shall see how the Body of Christ was built up, that temple made of living stones.

We shall see it all *as God sees it*. We shall see it perfectly because *we shall see God himself*. But this vision of God does not begin and end with what it means for the universe, for mankind, for history, on which our emphasis has been put. In the perfect harmony of joys of each and all, the vision will have for each one of us a yet deeper aspect of personal bliss and intimacy. For we shall not see God only as the beginning and end of his whole creation of nature and of grace: we shall see him *in himself and for himself*, in his inexhaustible and overflowing mystery. Entirely possessed by him, we shall possess God. Yes, *himself*!

Heaven is the object of our hope; but there is a foretaste and beginning of it in the life of faith on earth. As we have said, there are two aspects to this. First, the personal one, in the communion of faith and love which is the substance of spiritual life. Then, as regards the world: the world effectually healed and reconciled through Christian effort to give creation back its meaning, just that. God asks us to collaborate with him by striving for anticipations (however uncertain and weak they may be) of that which he himself will give us in its fullness when he exerts the power of his sovereignty—a restoration of wounded nature, of the distorted and broken image, a reconciliation of the world which, at present, knows him not and fights against him.

SOME PASSAGES FROM DOSTOEVSKY

To love somebody else as one loves oneself, which Christ told us to do—that is not possible. We are bound by the force of earthly personality: the 'me' stands in the way. Christ, and Christ alone, did it; but he was the eternal ideal, the ideal of the ages, to which man aspires and must aspire, impelled by nature.

Nevertheless, since Christ came to earth as man's ideal in the flesh, it has become as clear as daylight what the last and highest stage of the evolution of personality must be. It is this: that, when evolving is finished, at the very point where the end is reached, man finds out, understands and is convinced with all the force of his nature that the highest use he can make of his personality, of the full flowering of his *self*, is to do away with it, to give it wholly to any and everybody, without division or reserve. And that is sovereign happiness. Thus the law of 'me' is fused with the law of mankind; and 'I' and 'all' (in appearance two opposite extremes), each suppressing itself for the sake of the other, reach the highest peak of their individual development, each one separately.

That is exactly the paradise that Christ offers. The whole history of mankind, and of each individual man and woman, is simply an evolution towards, aspiration to, struggle for and achievement of this end.

But when this final end of mankind is attained there will be no further need to develop, to seek a realization of the ideal, to fight for it, to look forward to it amidst failures, to long to have it everlastingly—and consequently there will no longer be any need to live. Man on earth is only an evolving creature, that is, an incomplete, transitory being.

But it seems to me altogether pointless to achieve so great an object if, at the moment of success, everything is finished and done with, if life is at an end because its object is attained.

Therefore the future life, the life of Paradise, exists.

(From a note-book of Dostoevsky, published by B. Vycheslavtsev; tr. into French by X. Tilliette, *La légende du Grand Inquisiteur* . . ., Paris, 1958, pp. 60–61.)

Brothers, love the whole of God's creation, all of it, down to the very dust. Love each leaf, each ray of God's light. Love animals, love plants, love everything. If you love everything, you will understand the mystery of God in things. Once you see this, you will go on understanding it better every day. And eventually you will love the world with a love that includes every single thing. Love animals: God has given them a kind of thought and a tranquil enjoyment. Don't disturb it, don't hurt them, don't spoil their happiness, don't go contrary to God's purpose for them. Man, don't pride yourself on being above the animals: they are innocent creatures, but you defile the earth with your pride and leave a trail of filth behind you. Alas! it is true of nearly every one of us. Love little children especially, for they are as innocent as angels; they are given to us as a sign, to touch and cleanse our hearts. . . .

(From Father Zossima's conversations, in *The Brothers Karamazov*, bk. vi, ch. 3.)

'Dearest little mother, don't cry,' he would say, 'I'm going to live a long time yet, we shall be happy together, and life is so gay and jolly.'

'But, darling, what is there happy about tossing feverishly all night, coughing fit to tear yourself in pieces?'

'Mother, don't cry,' he would answer, 'Life is heavenly and we are all in Heaven, only we won't see it. If only we would, the whole world would be Heaven tomorrow morning.'

(*Ib.*, ch. 1.)

7

What Do We Know About Purgatory?

HERE again we have got to be careful what pictures we form in our minds. We cannot think without the help of images, they are useful and often fine; but there are at least certain flights of the imagination which must be got rid of.

From time to time preachers and writers have represented Purgatory as an organized torture-chamber. They tell us, for instance, of a freezing department, of a stream of molten metal, of a huge pot full of boiling oil. Tales are told of hands leaving a scorched print on wood or fabric—have then the *souls* in Purgatory got hands? In Rome there was once even a Museum of Purgatory, where such things could be seen; it was closed, it is said by order of the Holy Office. This authority would only have had to invoke a decree of the 25th session of the Council of Trent, which required bishops to prevent questionable particulars of Purgatory being given to the faithful, some of which details were superstitious.

Sometimes, again, Purgatory is spoken of in terms of days or years, as if it were a police-cell or a jail for criminals. Here there is a background image of pure punishment. If one had not read it for oneself, it would be unbelievable that such nonsense as the following should be written:

> Suppose that you are guilty every day of an average of ten faults; at the end of a year there will be a total of 3,650 faults—to simplify reckoning, say 3,000. At the end of ten years the total will be 30,000, after twenty years, 60,000.

Suppose that you expiate half of these 60,000 faults by repentance and good works; you then still have 30,000 to your debit. Continuing our hypothesis, you die at the end of these twenty years of virtuous life, and you appear before God owing a debt of 30,000 faults, which you have got to discharge in Purgatory. How long is this going to take?

Suppose that on an average each fault costs an hour of Purgatory. Judging by the revelations to some saints, this is very moderate, but say an hour. That makes 30,000 hours of Purgatory in all. Do you know how many years that comes to? Three years, three months and fifteen days. . . .[1] Why should not each fault earn a thrashing? That image would be quite in accord with this idea of a father-God with a big stick. But we need only think for a moment to realize that for souls in another life time is not measured as ours is, in days that mark the earth's rotation on itself or in years that mark its revolution round the sun. Purgatory has its own time, and that Purgatory is essentially a waiting is sufficient to make this time seem very long, not to say intolerably long.

Happily, the most authentic teachings on this subject are very different from the pictures given by tormented imaginations. The classic treatise of St Catherine of Genoa (d. 1510) does not contain a single word suggesting torments. It derives wholly from a true idea, a fruit of spiritual experience, of what God is and of what a soul who loves God is. 'After the happiness of the blessed in Heaven,' she writes, 'I do not believe there could be any happiness comparable with that of the souls in Purgatory' (ch. ii).[2] Catholic tradition is not without similar-sounding notes.

PURGATORY IN THE BIBLE AND TRADITION

The least that can be said is that the existence of Purgatory is implied and hinted at in the Bible, and this is seen yet more

[1] F. X. Schouppe, *Le dogme de Purgatoire* . . . (Paris, 1888), 93.
[2] A new translation into English of St Catherine's *Treatise on Purgatory* (with her Dialogue), made by Helen Douglas Irvine and Charlotte Balfour, was published in 1946.

clearly if we search the Scriptures in the way the Fathers did. That is, not in a narrowly juridical and literal spirit, that expects each statement to be materially supported by a formal reference (that attitude is, at bottom, secular-minded); but looking for 'sign-posts' to the sort of attitude required of us by the true religious harmony which should govern our life. Something more than a simple 'suggestion', but not necessarily a direct, formal statement; rather, a hint at what God wants us to do.

Now God wants us to pray for the dead, that, within the mystical Body, the living should help those who have gone before. That is shown in the story of Judas Machabaeus: after battle, heathen amulets were found on the bodies of dead Jewish soldiers, and Judas had atoning sacrifices offered for them, being convinced that the dead are purified between their death and the resurrection and are helped in this by the prayers of the living (2 Mach. xii. 39–46). An analogous conviction prompted the Christians at Corinth to do something for the dead, by 'being baptized for them' (1 Cor. xv. 29), though what exactly this means is far from clear.

The gospel of St Matthew xv. 25–26 and xii. 31–32, and of St Luke xii. 59, simply express the idea of having to pay one's debts in full. The commonest opinion of Catholic exegetes is that 1 Cor. iii. 10–15, with its rather obscure reference to fire, is not a direct testimony to Purgatory, though it lends itself to support of the doctrine. Doubtless St Paul is not speaking of Purgatory, but the Church's teaching can easily be written into his words and the ideas they suggest.

Special studies and the articles in standard works of reference give numerous quotations bearing on the doctrine, testifying to the chain of tradition. We will refer here to only one of these testimonies, the most beautiful, time-honoured and striking of them, and also one of the oldest. It is found in that remarkable document written in part by St Perpetua whilst in prison at Carthage, awaiting martyrdom. Her contribution, written in the first person, was finished the day before she and her companions were put to death; the martyrdom itself, which took place on 7 March 203, was described by another hand. Perpetua had had a brother who had died as a boy, probably without having been baptized. This is what she says of him:

A few days after [the martyrs' trial and conviction], while we were all praying, suddenly in the midst of the prayer I uttered a word and named Dinocrates; and I was amazed because he had never come into my mind save then; and I sorrowed, remembering his fate. And straightway I knew that I was worthy, and that I ought to ask for him. And I began to pray for him long, and to groan unto the Lord. Forthwith the same night, this was shown me.

I beheld Dinocrates coming forth from a dark place, where were many others also; being both hot and thirsty, his raiment foul, his colour pale; and the wound on his face which he had when he died. This Dinocrates had been my brother in the flesh, seven years old, who being diseased with ulcers of the face had come to a horrible death, so that his death was abominated of all men. For him therefore I had made my prayer; and between him and me was a great gulf, so that either might not go to other. There was moreover, in the same place where Dinocrates was, a font full of water, having its edge higher than was the boy's stature; and Dinocrates stretched up as though to drink. I was sorry that the font had water in it, and yet for the height of the edge he might not drink.

And I awoke, and I knew that my brother was in travail. Yet I was confident I should ease his travail; and I prayed for him every day till we passed over into the camp prison. (For it was in the camp games that we were to fight; and the time was the feast of Geta Cæsar.) And I made supplication for him day and night with groans and tears, that he might be given me.

On the day when we abode in the stocks, this was shown me.

I saw the place which I had before seen, and Dinocrates clean of body, finely clothed, in comfort; and the font I had seen before, the edge of it being drawn down to the boy's navel; and he drew water thence which flowed without ceasing. And on the edge was a golden cup full of water; and Dinocrates came up and began to drink therefrom; which cup failed not. And being satisfied he departed away from the water and began to play as children will, joyfully.

And I awoke. Then I understood that he was translated from his pains.[1]

Saint Perpetua, pray for us! Holy Church, pray for us!

MAKING SATISFACTION

The idea of punishment cannot be separated from the idea of sin, nor the idea of making amends from that of having committed offence against God. The link between these things is part of religious harmony as the Bible teaches us to live it, and is involved in the true idea of Christian repentance. Repentance, of course, is essentially *spiritual*, its essence is the turning of the heart *wholly* towards God; but repentance is serious only when it imposes a burden and proves itself by yielding 'acceptable fruit of repentance' (Luke iii. 8). The punishment which remains after we have been forgiven is less a retribution that God cannot do without (!) than the necessary and beneficial condition for the full reality of our turning to him.

It is true that Jesus has satisfied, 'made up', superabundantly for our sins and the sins of the world. But we are

---

[1] See *The Passion of SS. Perpetua and Felicity*, tr. and ed. by W. H. Shewring (London, 1931); the above passage is reproduced by kind permission of the publishers, Messrs Sheed & Ward. The testimony to Purgatory is not formal, but it is sufficient (cf. H. Leclercq in *Dict. d'archéol. chrét. et de liturgie*, vol. xiv, cc. 424ff.). For evidence of the commemoration of the dead and prayer for them in early Christianity, see *ib.*, vol. iv, cc. 427–56. That Dinocrates had not been baptized is suggested by his age, and especially by the fact that his sister and another brother had not yet been; their father was still a pagan (cf. the *Passio*, 2–3).

persons, not inanimate objects or creatures without responsibility. Nothing can be done for us unless we freely put our names to it. We have to 'enter into' those abounding amends that Jesus offered, just like the good works prepared for us of which it is written that 'we should walk in them' (Eph. ii. 10); and just like the Kingdom, which is made ready and offered, but we have still to 'enter in'. So also we have to enter into the satisfaction that Christ made, to enter into it in a living and personal way, by faith in the first place, but also by the works that must go with faith. The amends of the Body must follow those of the Head: amends *in Christ*, with Christ.

Amends are indeed made by the *Body:* first, by each of the members personally; but no one of them is alone, and all can help the others. The communion of saints is real. It is not, as some seem to fancy. a sort of childish book-keeping, in which the credit balances of good accounts are transferred for the benefit of bad accounts. The communion of saints is a Christian thing, and it is therefore spiritual and genuine, calling for a commitment of hearts. It brings together two complementary commands of the Bible: 'Every one shall bear his own burden' and 'Bear ye one another's burdens' (Gal. vi. 5, 2).

THE PLACE OF CLEANSING

'Penal satisfaction' is an essential element of Purgatory but not the most profound aspect. Purgatory is above all a place of *cleansing*.

There is nothing purifying about punishment that is simply submitted to and put up with. The punishments which God visits on his children despite his forgiveness, after his forgiveness, are purifying because they are accepted and acquiesced in. Those who pass through Purgatory are people who have appeared before God with a fundamental love of him in their hearts. That is why it can be said of them, as St Catherine of

Genoa said, and Cardinal Newman, that it is not so much God who banishes them from his sight; it is rather that the soul, seeing what it has been and is, flees from the face of God to seek a place where it will be made clean. It is in no state to receive the vision of God; as yet, it can see him only as its Burning Bush, and hear him say, 'Do not come nearer; rather take the shoes from thy feet [those shoes still muddy from their journeying], thou art standing on holy ground' (Exod. iii. 5). For it is a matter of nothing less than seeing God as he is, nothing less than becoming the place where God, being all in all, will assert himself and be fully God in us!

We indeed have to be made clean from all traces of sin, from its legacy that prevents us from being clear as crystal to God's shining rays. He is All; he is the Absolute; he is Holiness. However good our way to him, we have had to use relative means on that way: good things and activities of this world, a world of men and of created things. We have to disentangle ourselves from all that; the gold of our charity must be cleared of dross: we must be cleansed by fire.

This image, fire, is truly biblical; but there is nothing in the Bible, properly understood, nor in defined dogma that obliges us to hold that there is *material* fire in Purgatory, or that Purgatory is a *place* in the spatial sense of the word.[1]

It would certainly be much nearer the truth to see Purgatory as in line with those times and states of purification of their faith and love which are experienced by all religious people who are seriously treading the path of a total adherence to God. There are the crosses and disappointments whose object is to wean us from created things; earthly props are taken away so that we may lean wholly on God, and at first that is felt as a grievous deprivation; giving them up is bound to hurt. There is the farawayness of God whom we love, the

---

[1] See, e.g., P. Gasparri, *The Catholic Catechism* (London, 1934), pp. 457–8.

suffering from the barriers that still keep us from him: but all the time we are happy to be living as he wills, as St Catherine of Genoa used to stress so much. And then there is that kind of inward burning that comes from the soul feeling at the same time both God drawing it and the drag of its unworthiness because of sin. From Origen onwards, religious Christians have spoken of this fire that God kindles within them, a fire that burns the conscience. There can be no doubt that 'mystical purifications' provide one of the best illustrations for trying to understand Purgatory. They bring suffering; yet they are loved by those who undergo them, for they bring them nearer God and are a work of his mercifulness. 'In Purgatory we shall all be mystics.'

Origen again, and other Easterners after him, use a rather amusing illustration. They speak of a succession of *telonia*, custom-houses, in passing through which the traveller is relieved of the excess luggage and forbidden goods that hamper him on his journey to the Jerusalem that is above.

The purifying of the mystical Body is carried on and completed after its earthly existence. Its still uncleansed members experience as it were a sojourn in the tomb before that Easter of the world which will usher in the Lord's return, when there will be the coming out from the grave and the rising with Christ to God's right hand, where we are called to reign with him.

8

Hell Really Exists, But . . .

SALVATION saves me from being finally lost, from the possibility of being led by 'another' in a direction that he deceives me into thinking is for my good, but which in fact leads to death.

Who is this 'other'? The creature with horns and a tail that is shown in some pictures or in medieval carvings? Let us forget the horns and the tail, and any sort of physical imaginative representation—they are altogether too fanciful; what we need to do is to try and get a true idea of Hell and of the Devil, for that is necessary to a true idea of what it means to be saved.

Hell exists. The statements of God's word are so definite that we cannot question it.

The Jewish Bible often speaks of two things which together become part of the New Testament revelation: God's wrath against the wicked, and Sheol. Here is one text among many, referring to the unfaithful Israelites: 'The Lord was roused to anger when he saw it, saw his own sons and daughters defying him. I will turn away from them, he said. . . . My anger shall be like a raging fire that burns down to the depths of the abyss [Sheol]' (Deut. xxxii. 19–20, 22).

THE WORDS OF JESUS

The Jews gave the name 'Sheol' to that place beneath the earth which they believed was the abode of all the dead, without express distinction between the good and the wicked. Certain texts in our liturgy of the dead still use the word *infernus*, 'hell', in this general sense of a prison-like place, from which God is asked to free the dead; and the same sense is found in the Creed, when we say of Christ that he 'descended into hell'. Obviously there is no question of damnation here: Jesus went down 'into hell' full of love, and that is incompatible with damnation. It means that Jesus went into the very depths of death; and Scripture and the Fathers understand by this, not only bodily death, but that state of existence that no longer deserves to be called life. It is in this sense, to this depth, that Christ's resurrection is a rising *from among the dead*: Easter is the beginning of an integral salvation.

On the matter with which we are here concerned, Jesus and the Apostles affirm three things: (1) There will be a bodily resurrection of the good and of the wicked (John v. 29; Acts xxiv. 15); (2) Each one will reap the harvest of his deeds. After the time of mercy, giving opportunity for conversion to all, there will be a time of justice (1 Thess. i. 6–10; 1 Cor. vi. 9–10; Rom. ii. 5–11); (3) God's wrath will come in retribution upon the wicked, and, as in the Old Testament, that wrath is associated with fire (Matt. iii. 7; John iii. 36; Rom. ii. 5; 1 Thess. i. 10; and especially Heb. x. 26–31). The wicked will be accursed and reprobated: Hell is their place. Our Master, Jesus, the living Word of the true God, speaks of it in terms of 'outer darkness' and of Gehenna, 'the fires of Gehenna' (cf. Matt. v. 29, viii. 12, xxii. 13, xxv. 30 etc.). Perhaps the most terrible words our Lord ever uttered are those that come after his comforting words to the righteous for the Last Judgement: 'Go far from me, you that are accursed, into that eternal fire which has been prepared for the devil and his angels . . .' (Matt. xxv. 41).

So there is fire in Hell. That does not mean, however, that Hell is a sort of horrible oven, or that, as the men of old thought, its fire is vomited out at the surface of the earth by volcanoes. We speak of fire because it is the most intensely painful of the elements; but Hell's fire burns without consuming. We must get an idea of this fire befitting what it represents: it is something real as regards the body, but it is fundamentally spiritual; for, again and always, it is a matter of God and his rational creature, and of the relation existing between them when it is no longer possible for the creature to turn away from his sin, and only God's justice and wrath are left.

We must, then, put away our copy of *The Divine Comedy*. We must strive for a spiritual picture of Hell. Not by philosophizing—the dogma excludes a purely inward interpretation, as if the fire were simply the feeling of remorse, for instance. Not by philosophizing, then, but through truth.

THE ABSOLUTE BEING AND FINITE BEINGS

The subject of Hell is a part of theology, not of dramatic art. It expresses one aspect of man's spiritual relationship with God, but man is body as well as soul. And here is a first point, of the highest importance: Hell was not willed for its own sake. *There is no predestination to Hell* (against Calvin). God has made nothing *for* destruction or *for* unhappiness. Hell is to be understood in the setting of a wholly positive pattern, contained in the proposal and offer of a covenant; we can then see that it results from the full truth and momentousness of what is offered and of the parties to the covenant.

For his part, God offers a communion, a fellowship, which embraces total salvation, so that to reject or lose it entails total loss. God is Goodness; but he is also the Absolute, sovereign Act. He is not at all the indulgent grandpa who can always be won over in the end. An invitation to a covenant with the living God is an infinitely serious matter. It is an expression of his will; and, if it be ignored or refused, that expression does not disappear into thin air and become as if it had never existed. God's will continues, as a command. It may be scorned or simply disregarded, but it will infallibly produce its effects; and those things that were intended for our benefit will turn to our shame. God wanted to join us to him and to shower kindness on us; instead, we come under his sway as empty and beaten men. That idea accords with tradition, it is biblical, St Paul has it—the idea that those who do not come to God's reign by the way of mercy will do so by the way of justice. 'Those who do not yield to his goodness now will find out his power at the day of Judgement': so wrote St Irenaeus, and he quotes Rom. ii. 4–6.

God being absolute, perfect and infinite Being, how can there be finite beings? Plenty of philosophers have engaged their minds on this mystery. It is clear that, since finite beings only exist through infinite Being, they must return to him. The French philosopher Lachelier saw here the foundation, or even the fundamental nature, of sacrifice: 'The basis of sacrifice seems to be that the finite subsists only provisionally outside the infinite, as it were on sufferance; and that it seems fitting to the finite itself to relinquish this toleration.' The finite being *must* be restored to the absolute Being: *it is so ordered*. And he who does not return freely in obedience to love will be constrained to do so.

On man's side, there is the immensely important business of freedom. The biblical message and Christian dogma presuppose the reality of this freedom, otherwise they would be absurd. I can say 'No' to God. I can literally stand up to him. 'I tilt with God. . . . Within me there is the capacity, if not the right, to counterbalance him' (M. Jouhandeau). Yes, he lets me go as far as that!

This present life is very definitely a time of choice. Its conditions are to live in a human body, in time, and, to the extent that we have to decide the direction our life shall take, we do

73

so within the limits and according to the circumstances imposed by these two conditions. Since we never know more than a limited aspect of things, and different aspects at different times, we can change our minds: even when we believe and intend our choices to be irrevocable, they never are so— except when God himself makes them permanent with his own steadfastness. Life in the body and existence in time determine man's state as one in which he is able to change his direction, in a word, to be converted, in one sense or another. So there are three things we have to take into account on this earth: a Church which in its most authentic aspect is the communion of saints; a world in the sense of our Lord's words 'The world hates me'; and a world in the neutral sense, the framework for the free use we are called to make of our liberty.

When earthly time ends for us, when the soul ceases to give life to its body and leaves it, we enter into another time, which has different conditions: an order of things in which (account being taken of Purgatory) there is no neutral middle term but simply Kingdom and anti-Kingdom, life or death, salvation or banishment. Our freedom is fixed. However poor our use of it may have been—God knows our weakness—it is fixed just as death finds it, whether turned Godward or against him. When Bossuet wrote that 'Hell is sin itself', he meant that fundamentally Hell is simply the bringing home to us of the consequence of an attitude taken up during the time when we were free to choose one. In the same way, Barbey d'Aurevilly said that 'Hell is Heaven in reverse', and a contemporary Anglican theologian, Dr E. L. Mascall, has declared that God's anger is simply God's love as it shows itself to a sinner. The sinner is, by definition, one who does not love God; and to such a one, God's love is merely a contradiction and, since God's love is mighty and burning, its contradiction is hard and bitter.

Hell is not a 'shilling shocker' or a 'terror' film. It is something real that follows from the nature of God and the nature of man, in their deepest and most significant aspects. And this is well worth noticing: that contemporary thought, even the thought of unbelievers, when it searches the depths of spiritual being and freedom, arrives at a conception of Hell which is far from being superficial; and this even when, ignoring God and the majesty of God and therefore the meaning of sin, man alone is considered.[1] A recent inquiry by the French Institute of Public Opinion found that, among people of from 18 to 30 years of age, 40 per cent believe that they will again meet their loved ones after death, and 38 per cent believe in a paradise, a purgatory and a hell.

The inquiry does not state *what* hell. We have begun an answer to the question from the point of view of an authentically Christian theology. But we are well aware that there still remain serious and difficult questions. Two of them are particularly important: How should the aspect of punishment, especially fire, be represented to ourselves? Is man really so free that he can end up in *that*?

HELL FIRE

We have known since our catechism days that Hell's punishments involve the pain of *loss* and the pain of *sense*; that the first consists in being deprived of God, and that the second is felt by the body (and by the soul too, since it exists in Hell before the resurrection of the body). The reflections which follow will enable us to understand that there is a close bond between these two kinds of suffering; and that the bodily punishments, far from being a sort of arbitrary addition to the already total punishment of damnation, must be understood

[1] I have in mind such writers as M. Jouhandeau, *Algèbre des valeurs morales*, N. A. Berdyaev, *The Fate of Man in the Modern World* (London, 1935) and in U.S.A. *The Destiny of Man* (Harper Torchbooks, 1959), J. P. Sartre, *Les Mouches* and *Huis-Clos* trans. *No Exit and three other plays* (Knopf, U.S.A., 1956) and Dostoevsky.

fundamentally as deriving from that, as a consequence from its principle.

To be damned is to be cut off from God. If holiness consists in living in and with God, damnation is the uttermost limit of the contrary, existence apart from God—not beyond his power, for nothing exists beyond his power, but outside his fellowship and his love. If Heaven is 'God all in all', then Hell is God in nothing and nobody. I have willed to lead my life without God, or against him. Or, without willing that directly, I have wanted to lead it only for myself, at the risk of not doing it for him and of doing it against him. And then I reach the end, my life is finally reckoned up, its fruits are ripe for picking and eating—and I find myself indeed without God, excluded from the God whom I have excluded from my life.

The further punishment is one that I feel in my body because I am a living corporeal being. Nothing is significant and complete for man unless it arouses echoes in his body. God himself, when he loves man 'even to the end,' gives himself to him in bodily form: he takes human flesh, he establishes a sacrament of body and of blood.

Holy Scripture speaks of this physical punishment chiefly in two sets of concrete terms. First, in terms of a prison: it is like a deep pit, an underground cistern, an abyss into which one falls; it is a dungeon into which one is cast, bound hand and foot; the door is well bolted and barred. Thick darkness reigns there.[1] Then, in terms of flames: the fires of Gehenna, the fiery lake, the fire that is never quenched.[2] Probably the two sets of images are meant to be understood so far as possible as representing a single reality: something like a prison with

[1] For the Old Testament, see Isa. xxxviii. 10, 18; Ps. xxvii. 1, 29; 4; Prov. i. 12; Job x. 20ff., xvii. 16, xxxviii. 17; for the New Testament, 2 Pet. ii. 4, 17; Jude vi. 13; Apoc. xx. 1–3; for 'outer darkness', Matt. viii. 12, xxii. 13, xxv. 30.
[2] Matt. v. 22, xviii. 8–9, xxv. 41; Mark ix. 44–46; Apoc. xix. 20, xx. 10, 14–15.

walls of flame, a place and state that destroys freedom and happiness, as a prison does, and that is searing, as fire is. It is thus, after much groping and hesitation due to incurable lack of knowledge, that theologians of the stature of St Thomas Aquinas have believed themselves able to understand a tiny bit of what, when all is said and done, remains a mystery for us.

We have to find a way between two extremes: between a sort of 'fundamentalism',[1] a heavy-handed literalism that makes Hell a furnace that is as shocking as it is unthinkable to the mind, and a symbolical interpretation that is far too 'spiritualizing', an interpretation that is opposed by the Church's teaching authority and by patristic and theological tradition. It is a good thing to overhaul our religious mental images;[2] indeed, it is necessary to do so if those images are not to be altogether too unworthy of God, of ourselves, and of the religious relationship in which the divine purpose consists. But, in criticizing the more or less pictorial expressions of Revelation, we must not whittle down positive statements to make them fit only what is clear to human reason.

So we will think of the fire as being something real outside ourselves; just as prison walls are not only the despair that makes us feel our situation is hopeless—we are also actually up against something hard and high, hemming us in on every side.

But we also will remember what theology has to say to us. Fire? There are other pains of Hell, but they are summed up in this one as being the most tormenting, the extreme example of what hurts. The Church has not defined anything concerning the nature and action of this fire, not even its physical

---

[1] *Fundamentalism:* an attitude of mind which, starting from a rather material conception of biblical inspiration, applies the least text of Scripture with a rigidity that does not take into consideration either the literary forms or the aims of the sacred writings: for example, a whale is said really to have swallowed a prophet named Jonas (Jonah).
[2] Nowadays we often hear of 'demythologizing': it means the criticism of certain presentations of the Christian message in such a way as to make its content acceptable to the scientifically-minded of our time.

reality. In any hypothesis, it is fire of another world than ours, for it burns without consuming its object or itself. Those who, like St Thomas (and unlike St Bonaventure), attribute true physical reality to it, are upholding an idea that is well consonant with Scripture; the fire, they say, is an instrument of God's wrath and God's justice. We should fix our attention, not so much on the fire itself and its ability to burn, as on what *God* is doing: he is punishing and, in the event, using fire for that purpose.[1]

HELL IS MEANINGLESS EXISTENCE

The man who is damned is not alone. He belongs to and lives in a world of sorts. But this world, and the other people who are there with him, and his own existence are simply prison and pain; he is committed to a world and an existence that are meaningless; he knows it, and he knows that nothing can be done about it. It is of the essence of this fire that it should not destroy what it burns. To be damned is to be irrevocably bound to an existence and to other beings and to a whole world in which the meaning of being and of existing is unalterably absent. It is to be henceforth dependent only on God's power, not on his grace. There is, as it were, a 'stuff of things' proper to Heaven, to earth and to Hell: that of Heaven is love, fellowship and the effects of graces; that of earth is faith and hope, the possibility that things will go better tomorrow, the possibility of conversion; but that of Hell is an unchanging, unending existence without meaning and without hope. Dostoevsky—again!—wrote penetratingly on all this (see below, p. 82).

The famous 'damned in this world' deserved the name in another and deeper sense than Pottier suspected, for they were indeed without God and their life was without hope or mean-

[1] For this section, see St Thomas, *Sent.* iv, d.44, q.3, a.2, 1; *Suppl.*, q.70, a.3; q. 97,, a.1, 1, and a.5.

ing. Saint-Exupéry is right: 'The free man is he who finds a meaning in his work.' Equally with his material conditions, a man is free or enslaved, feels happy or miserable, accordingly as he does or does not find meaning in his life and particularly in his work. Listen to Saint-Exupéry again:

> We want to be set free. The man who wields a pickaxe wants to know the meaning of what he is doing; and a convict's pick stroke, which humiliates him, is not the same as a prospector's pick stroke, which stimulates the prospector. Penal servitude is not working with a pickaxe, it is not the physical hardship. Penal servitude is when one's pick strokes have no meaning, when they do not unite the striker with the human community.

Now the man who is damned goes on existing and cannot cease to do so, yet he has for ever lost, and knows that he has lost, the meaning of his existence and, with it, the truth of his being: he has in a way been sentenced to go on living without any meaning in doing so. In such conditions, life is a prison, penal servitude; we sometimes call it 'a veritable hell'. Unfortunately, thoughtless as we are, we also call it 'a real calvary', whereas Calvary is the very opposite of hell, for it overflows with love and the fullest significance of sacrifice. Hell's suffering, on the contrary, hurts in the full measure that it is imposed and undergone, not willed and offered as a sacrifice, and it is in consequence powerless to cleanse; it hurts, then, in the full measure that it has no meaning and that one cannot give it one through sacrifice—for to do that one would have to love God, and to love God would be to come out of Hell. The very recognition of Christ's lordship, which is such that at his name every knee must bend—the very recognition of this is without meaning in Hell, for it is compelled and joyless.

In Hell, meaningless existence goes on endlessly, it is sustained yet as it were destroyed, both at once. In Taziev's film

Les rendez-vous du diable we were shown the volcano ceaselessly built up and demolished, added to and lessened; and, at a photograph of Etna in full eruption, this was well expressed by the words 'a mixture of creation and end of the world'. The Redemption is just the opposite: it maintains the Creation as well as the Covenant, in spite of sin; it is the offer made anew, the restoration of meaning to man's life and the world's, notwithstanding the sinfulness that normally only incurs God's anger and devastation, as we see in the story of the Flood and of Sodom. Hell, says the liturgy, is the place where there is no Redemption. . . .

. . . Unless God chose to start a quite new chapter after all this, about which he would not have given us a single word.[1] This could come to doing away with Hell. But *revelation as it has been delivered to us* speaks, and through the mouth of Jesus himself, of eternal fire and of eternal punishment (Matt. xviii. 8, xxv. 41, 46).

We will venture a kind of parable. Jesus spoke of Heaven in parables (a great supper, a wedding feast); can we not then think of its infernal counterpart as the state of a child who has incurred and provoked his parents' anger? The child has no other roof, no other table; he is part of a household, which at this moment however is no longer a home to him; everything seems upside down to him, unsettled, hostile, with no way out: for the tie of dependence and affection on which his happiness depends is no longer there. The world of the man who is damned is rather like that: created things, other people, his own life, all are hostile to him; and he is powerless to escape. That is not a home to live in, it is a prison. All that hostility is a

---

[1] Were we not dispensed from completeness, we should have to mention here a doctrine that had its supporters among the Fathers and in the middle ages, and to which ancient liturgical texts testify: namely, that God in his mercy mitigates the pains of Hell at the prayer of the faithful (see *Dict. de théol. cath.*, s.v. Mitigation). Good works done here below can also obtain an abatement (St Thomas, III, q.89, a.6, ad.3).

torment; at all points of his bodily and spiritual existence, the outcast feels the aggregate of things to which he is bound like a gnawing, burning despair, the Gehenna of fire. That fire is real, not purely psychological and moral—but it is not the fire of a roasting spit, with little horned demons turning the handle.

God is not a torturer. He is God. The Bible and theology say that his punishments are less than the sinner deserves.[1] But where he is not, there is damnation; he is there as creator, but not as the living God, the God of the Covenant, except through the dreadful emptiness that bears witness to his absence. Damnation is that abyss.

HELL IS THE HARVEST OF SIN

If they are sound, these explanations enable us to understand a little less inadequately what sin and salvation are: the first step towards damnation, and its opposite.

Sin is wherever God is not, the things to which we do not give the meaning that God wishes, whatever God is kept out of. In the end, unless it has been wiped out by repentance and forgiveness—a real repentance and forgiveness which puts God back into life and again conforms action to the meaning he wishes it to have—in the end, sin is Hell, as Bossuet said.

On the other hand, as we have seen, salvation is essentially the giving of meaning to life—its real meaning, its meaning in God's eyes, for there is no other that is true and all-embracing. To be saved is to be snatched from an existence that is meaningless, hopeless and doomed to unending death. To be saved is for existence to have the meaning that Jesus gave to it and, by that very fact, to have the assurance of everlasting life, body and soul, there where everything will be meaningful,

[1] God is slow to anger, rich in mercy, yet a stern judge: cf. Exod. xxxiv. 6–7; Ps. cii. 8, 17–18, cxliv. 8; Joel ii. 13; 1 John iv. 8–10; and many other places. It is a commonplace of theology that God punishes less and rewards more than our deserts; cf. *Sum. theol.*, I, q.21, a.4, ad 1.

where the joyous perception of the meaning of things will be savoured with a delight infinitely exceeding the joys of this world. And so we shall give thanks.

DOSTOEVSKY ON HELL

What is Hell? It is the suffering that comes from being unable to love. Once in the infinite existence that cannot be measured in time or space, a spiritual creature, appearing on earth, was given the ability to say 'I am and I love'. Once, and only once, he was given a moment of active, living love, and it was for that that he received earthly life, with its temporal limitations. But that happy being did not appreciate and welcome the priceless gift; he rejected it, looking at it perversely and unmoved. Such a one, on leaving the earth, sees the place where Abraham is and talks with him, as in the parable of Dives and Lazarus; he beholds Heaven and can go up to God. But it is precisely in that that his torment lies: to go loveless before God, to draw near to those who have loved, when he has despised their love. For he sees clearly, and he says to himself: 'Now I understand. But, though I now long to love, my love can be worth nothing, there can be no sacrifice in it, for earthly life is behind me. Abraham will not come with a drop of living water (that is the gift of the earthly active life that is over) to quench the burning thirst for spiritual love that now devours me, though in life I despised it. There is no more life for me, and no more time! Now I would gladly give my life for others; but it cannot be, for the life which can be sacrificed for love is gone, and there is a great gulf between it and my existence now.

People talk about the material fire of Hell. It makes me shudder, and I do not pry into that mystery. But I think that, were the fire material, the damned would really be glad of it; for I imagine that physical suffering would enable them to forget their still greater spiritual suffering, if only for a moment. And that spiritual suffering cannot be taken away, for it is caused from within them, not from outside. . . .

In Hell there are some who remain proud and cruel in spite of their certain knowledge and sight of the unavoidable truth; there are some terrifying ones who have wholly given themselves up to Satan and his proud spirit. They have chosen Hell and can never have their fill of it; their state is of their own choosing. They cursed God in life, and now are themselves accursed. They feed on their malignant pride like a man starving in the desert who sucks blood from his own veins. But they can never have enough, never, and they spurn forgiveness, cursing the God who calls them. They cannot look upon the living God without hating him and they wish that the God of life could be no more, that he would destroy himself and all his creation. They will burn eternally in the flames of their own rage, longing for death and nothingness. But there will be no death for them.

(From Father Zossima's conversations, in *The Brothers Karamazov*, bk. vi, ch. 3.)

9

To Lose All or to Win All:
Are We Really Free Enough?

THERE is ascribed to Abbé Mugnier a sally to the effect that 'Hell exists, but it is nearly empty'. People are not free enough to be so wicked as to deserve it. Poor people! When we look at them and consider the physiological or economic conditionings to which they are subject, the social pressure, the 'super-ego' overbearing and stifling the 'me', bad heredity, bad or deficient education, the fact of the subconscious and unconscious that excite urges within us, lead to complexes, and muddy the clearness of our processes—when we consider these things, it is enough to make us put a big question-mark against every paean to human freedom.

And then, how often, except in very rare cases, do these same unfortunate people have sufficient grasp of the matters at issue to be really responsible for refusing the covenant that God offers them in Jesus Christ? Must we not admit that the question seems never to present itself to many of them? And when it does, is it not so distorted and mixed up with other things that they do not recognize it? So they miss the main point, and lay their course according to some detail or other of the surface web of life.

It is not necessary to recognize God to be able to reject or to love him. There is the answer of the Gospel. Our question is found on our Lord's own lips: 'When was it that we saw thee hungry, or thirsty, or a stranger, or naked, or sick, or in prison, and did not minister to thee?' (Matt. xxv. 44). The damned protest and ask questions, for they are not conscious of having ever had—if one may dare say it—the chance to take sides against God. The Gospel answer is of immense significance, and we shall come back to it when we consider the salvation of those to whom the Gospel has not been announced. God does not of necessity present himself for our free choice with face unveiled. He even cannot do so, for it would be to constrain our freedom of choice: so glorious would be his beauty, so overwhelming the evidence that here is absolute Good, that it would not be possible to refuse him. That freedom of choice of ours requires that God should be as it were disguised, that there should be a certain ambiguity, a kind of half-light. But it is necessary that we see sufficiently well in this twilight for us to be responsible for making a decision *against*. . . .

ENDLESS PUNISHMENT FOR PASSING SIN?

Revelation tells us that Hell lasts for ever. It is a matter of final and irreparable loss, of a debt that *nothing* can wipe out. Is that possible? Surely my misdeeds are transient? Even the more serious ones will have lasted only for a time. Can a moment's misdoing receive an unalterable punishment?

Let us just look at 'punishment'. First of all we must dismiss any notion that would make God a torturer and Hell an organization of endless torments. So far as a punishment has to make up for the disorderliness of our corrupt, materialistic, self-indulgent use of created things, there can be question only of a limited punishment, proportionate to the offence committed. It is unthinkable, it would be blasphemous, to suppose that God punishes a limited disorder by unlimited retribution, or that he attaches an equal penalty to transgressions that are unequal. On the other hand, there is an element common to all sin, present equally in all real sin, namely, a turning away from God, saying 'No' to him. And the grievousness of this is infinite. To a questioner to whom he wanted to bring home the necessity of a ransom of equally infinite worth, St Anselm said 'You have not yet realized the full gravity of sin!' (*Cur Deus homo*, 1, 21).

The fact is that we do not fully realize it because we have a very weak feeling for God's majesty and the boundless demands of his holiness. We are sensible enough to what touches us; we are moved by the aspect of a sin that wrongs us, or does harm to others. In however small a degree, we are touched by the thought of what sin cost the perfectly Righteous One; the women of Jerusalem wept over Jesus, staggering, bruised, under the weight of his cross:

> 'Weep for yourselves,' said Jesus.
> And so we do,
> but at our disappointments
> and not for our misdeeds.
>
> (Henri Ghéon)

We do not weep over our sins and failings because we do not appreciate the gravity of sin as an offence committed *against God*. And this is so because we do not appreciate the holy majesty of God. It is significant that the saints, who appear so good to us, looked on themselves as dreadful sinners. People who go to confession once a year, if that, and never examine their conscience, do not see anything to accuse themselves of; they have done no evil, they have not failed to do good. That is to be expected: they are not living in God's presence; the all-holy God, with his supreme demands, is not the greatest reality in their lives. Only saints know what sin is, because they know what God is. They are not surprised that final separation from the living God should be the penalty for behaviour that has ignored and flouted his majesty. They know that sin is deadly to the soul, and that death may indeed follow: that death which, we have seen, is not annihilation but the endless continuance of an existence that has lost its meaning.

Can one go to Hell for a single deadly sin? Surely it is difficult to think so when we look at man's obvious weakness, his blindness, the waverings of his will. Can he or can he not be lost for ever because of one real sin?

If one insists on putting the question in this form, the answer must be Yes, he can. But it is a very bad way of putting it, for it is so abstract—in the strongest sense of the word—that it verges on the unreal. To put the question this way is to ignore its 'existential' conditions. The human condition, bound as it is to the body, is such that it knows no decision that is wholly pure, once-for-all, irrevocably bringing about a destiny. Our conscious life is a flowing stream, a whole, in which moments of decision are (miracle or catastrophe apart) related to what has gone before, to what accompanies them, and to what follows them. Our eternal lot is decided existentially by our life as a whole, it is that which accepts or rejects God and the invitation (in whatever form it takes) he extends to us to enter into fellowship with him. We shall see later on the scope of 'whatever form it takes'.

If the question be put at the level of particular actions, certainly few of them will be found wholly free among most people, and fewer still that are weighty enough to represent a choice of eternal destiny. But man must be considered at another level, at that of the inner direction of his life, however inadequate the life, whether it be directed to himself only or to something outside self. Man is not completely determined by nature, he is not exclusively what nature's conditions make him, unlike the lower animals, which are not able themselves to modify the behaviour whose mechanism comes to them with life itself. Man has been given a nature that is pretty narrowly conditioned; but it is *he* who determines the *use* to be made of it, if not in this or that particular case, yet in a general sense and fundamental direction. His existence, therefore, is not simply something given that pushes him on, but a task to do with which he is confronted.

It is true that the inward choice has in the end to be made at the level of certain actions. But, on the one hand, it is a matter of the fundamental direction involved in a mass of lesser decisions, in the whole use a man makes of his existence. And on the other hand, there are in every life, unless one is insane or hopelessly deranged, moments when there is an opportunity for generous choice, when a person's course for the future is bound up with eternal destiny, perhaps at one stroke or at any rate for the most part. Examples could be given from the lives of the saints: the meeting of Francis of Assisi with the leper, or Teresa Martin's chance to 'enjoy a bit of life' during the months before going into Carmel. Other examples could be taken from cases of psychic disorder: for, beside those blameless sufferers whose psychosis originates in an organic ailment, there are those whose illness is due to a responsible (if not fully conscious) reaction to some disappointment or trouble—things could have taken a different turn had rancour or selfishness not been given in to.

Between the two, the saints and the sick, we may refer to an example related by Albert Camus in *La chute*. Not that Camus himself is an ideal reference for us; we find his frankness rather corroding and his criticism rather barren. But the case on which he uses his recognized ability is a striking one: a decent man, of good position and respected socially, one day fails to go to the help of a drowning girl. His life goes on afterwards against its background of respect and outward success; but it has now been poisoned at its source, reduced to the lowest level of human inadequacy, without kindness or nobility. The man does not even want to alter it, and the story ends with these words: 'Young woman, throw yourself into the water again, so that I may have a second chance to save us both!... But cheer up! It is too late now, and it will always be too late—happily!'

In the world of Camus there will be no second chance, because there is no God in quest of our souls; and that accounts for the bitter irony of this hopeless ending. In reality it does not happen that a missed opportunity of ransoming oneself and choosing courageously is not offered a second time, and a third. Earthly life is lived in time, and time is given us precisely that we may undergo conversion, that we may, in biblical terms, repent and 'do penance'. In some form or another, it is always a matter of choosing to be generous and to go beyond oneself (and that is hard for a selfish person); it is a choice of real *love*.[1] Call it sacrifice. Sacrifice is the outstanding sign of freedom; it is at the same time freedom's infallible teacher and marks the highway to it.

Man is an animal who is able to make a sacrifice.

A THEOLOGIAN'S HYPOTHESIS

Mgr Palemon Glorieux, former rector of the Catholic university at Lille, has put forward an hypothesis enabling the critical choice, which we see expressed through a whole life that includes several special occasions, to be thought of in the form of a definite free act, 'made in broad daylight'. According to this hypothesis, the moment of death would allow the possibility of a choice which, for many people, could be the first really understanding and free choice they would make, having until then been much more conditioned and driven than in a fit state to choose. This moment cannot be *after* death—that would be too late—but at the point of existence which still belongs to bodily life, whilst touching, tangentially as it were, the instant when the chance of freedom will be gone.

[1] Read again the passage from Dostoevsky on p. 82, above.

Theologians have shown reserve about this hypothesis. There is no need to evoke a sort of positive and optimistic complement to what we rejected just now in the idea of damnation for a single deadly sin, without reference to the concrete conditions of earthly existence, transferring the counterpart to a man's last moment. Of course there can be sudden inpourings of grace at that moment, and they are by definition 'gratuitous'. St John Vianney assured the distraught widow of a suicide that her husband had, between the parapet and the river, received the grace of repentance and therefore of conversion. Were one to accept the hypothesis of a finally understanding and free choice at the hour of death, it would be necessary to think, ordinarily, of a sort of totalling up of the fundamental choices of life.

> Each sinner [wrote Origen in the third century] kindles for himself the flame of his own fire. . . . The fuel of this fire is our sins, which feed it. It seems to me that, just as too much food or its bad quality produces fevers in the body . . . so the soul heaps up sins and misdeeds, and in due course this accumulation of wickedness catches fire in retribution and flares up in punishment. (*De principiis*, ii, 10, 4–5.)

It must be admitted that such considerations do not throw much light on the mystery. It would be very nearly useless to offer them to anyone who does not believe in God or who does not love him. It requires a very strong conviction of the holiness, the majesty, the justice and the goodness of God, all together, to enable one unswervingly to hold the doctrine of Hell, understanding the doctrine in its authentic form, as spiritual and purged from all its trimmings of the torture-chamber.

THE ALL-HOLY GOD IS THE DECISIVE FACTOR

We must go still farther. The difficulty—and we do not want to minimize its weightiness—is presented within the limitations of a consideration of man *only*; and therefore, once again, it is taken out of the real existential conditions in which it ought to be looked at. For there is the decisive factor in the problem which objection does not take into account—God, God the holy, God the just, God the good, the living God of whom all Revelation, consummated in Jesus Christ, tells us that he is inseparably justice and mercy. He it is who has made us, and he knows from what dust of the earth we are made, and how the spiritual spark with which he has endowed us is a weak and wavering thing, at the same time that it is a reflection beyond price of the divine countenance. He knows what it is in us that refuses or accepts him, and under what disguises he has asked us for a little love, and we have not pierced them. He is the master of history, and he knows on what warp we have been called humbly to weave our lives. The choice deep down within us, which is so murky and uncertain to us—he knows that too, he gives it its true name, it is he who has inspired all that is good in it. He will not be deceived in judging what it is worth.

Reader, you will not be judged by men, but by your Creator and Redeemer. Do not be afraid.

TWO CONSIDERATIONS ON OUR FREEDOM

Two considerations can be of help in taking the measure of a freedom which we begin to question only when there is danger of its leading us into tragedy. First, the tragedy is not simply in some future, and so far away that we can always put off thinking about it till tomorrow: it is with us now, it has already happened. It is Jesus Christ taking on himself, with his cross, the world's sin and dying of that sinfulness. When we look at Jesus on his cross, we become conscious of how really sin banishes God from the world. However inadequate our freedom may be, it is strong enough to do that. . . . It carries so much weight that this price had to be paid.

And it carries so much weight that it can gain Heaven, that is, fellowship with God and the fulfilment of our life's meaning, perfectly blissful, satisfying and joyous. Our freedom may be very circumscribed and mutable; but we shall more easily understand that it is able to lose all for us if we see it, as it really is, able to win all for us.

IO

No Salvation Outside the Church?

I THE HISTORY OF A FORMULA

AMONGST 'the others', the question of whose salvation disturbs us, are the numberless people who have not known Jesus Christ, or even perhaps the existence of God. We know now that milliards of people lived and died before a word of God had been uttered to them, for man appeared on earth more than 500,000 years before our father Abraham. Even today, what is the position of the Christian faith in the world, statistically speaking? If salvation depends on the meaning given to one's life in relation to God and Jesus Christ, where does the famous 'milliard of heathen' of our missionary exhibitions stand with regard to salvation?—a milliard that is more than that, and gets more every day. At this very moment, nearly one man in every four is Chinese; it is said that a new Chinese is born every second of the day: what becomes of these little Chinese?

To talk about the salvation of 'the others' is too vague. Shall we say 'non-Catholics' then? But the problem applies to many who have been baptized Catholics, some of whom are Catholics by practice. It would be an understatement to say that many are not Christians. Are *we*? Yes, in the sense that to be Christian is, not to have become it—that can never be achieved—but consists in trying to become it. Nevertheless, François Mauriac's statement is true: 'Most Christians have never got beyond the letter of the catechism, they have not known God. It is a word that has no real meaning for them. They ignore him without denying him. . . .' Mauriac is speaking of the baptized and instructed; but in France, as in England, large numbers of our brethren in destiny are neither the one nor the other. Shall we then say 'unbelievers' or, using a more comprehensive expression, 'people without faith'? But if it be admitted that they can be saved, we know that this cannot be so without faith, in whatever form that faith exists psychologically (we shall come back to that). So these people are not unbelievers or 'without faith'. . . .

The best way to formulate the question is as 'the salvation of those who are not evangelized'. This expresses their indubitable and acknowledged state, without in any way prejudging their moral position. The problem then is: What can one reasonably think about the eternal lot of those who on this earth have known nothing of Jesus Christ, nor even perhaps of God?

One may refuse to answer this question, or even to ask it, on the ground that Revelation tells us nothing about the subject. That is a position fairly generally taken by Eastern Orthodox and Protestants. It is perhaps a rather easy way of excusing oneself from an inquiry that is legitimate and may be called for. Is it certain that Revelation tells us nothing, if not formally, at least in the implications that emerge when we study the hints, compare the texts and consider whither they lead? One thing is certain anyway: the question has been discussed at times all through the history of Christian thought. Whether we like it or not, we are all born heirs of a past; and to make an inventory of the past is the beginning of development in any field. To draw up the history of a question is often to begin the understanding of it. We will attempt it then. We shall find that the history of our problem contains some extremely interesting lessons and that, if we wish to draw a conclusion, they are remarkably apposite today.

No Salvation Outside the Church?

Is there any formula more well known than 'Outside the Church there is no salvation'? It would not be difficult to find equivalents to it in the New Testament; but it is found for the first time in its present form, two examples of it at the same moment, about the year 250, on the pen of two confessors of the faith whom one cannot know without loving, Origen at Alexandria and St Cyprian at Carthage. Applying the words to people who live after Christ's coming, they mean them in an absolute, exclusive sense. It would be necessary to go into careful detail and make distinctions were we writing learnedly and scientifically; but we are not doing that, and it is enough for us to quote, as representative of this way of understanding the formula, these words of a disciple of St Augustine, St Fulgentius of Ruspe (d. 533): 'It cannot be doubted that, not only all pagans, but also all Jews, heretics and schismatics, who die outside the Catholic Church, will go to that eternal fire which has been prepared for the Devil and his angels' (*De fide ad Petrum*, 38, 79).

It is important to notice that the bishop of Ruspe understands 'Outside the Church . . .' in a way that *applies it to persons*; he does not name them individually—no Catholic has ever done that!—but he mentions their chief categories. It is not that Fulgentius or Augustine or Cyprian were harder-hearted than we are. They believed that there is no salvation except through Christ, and we believe the same with them. But they did not see any way of honouring this fundamental principle other than by excluding from salvation those men who had known nothing of Jesus Christ or had denied and rejected the means instituted by him to carry his salvation to the world, namely, the Church. The whole question turns on this point: is there or is there not another way of honouring the principle of the oneness of the mediator of salvation?

The Fathers, and the middle ages after them, knew that

not only were there Jews, heretics and schismatics mingled with Catholics in Christian lands, but also that there were other peoples, beyond the frontiers of where the Church had taken root. In the middle ages they were popularly called Ethiops, 'Blacks'. People credited the fable of the existence of creatures half-man and half-dog, such as are represented over the doorway of the church at Vézelay. Those who were better informed could have some idea of what missionaries, such as Ascelin and John of Plano Carpini, had come across in Persia and Turkestan.

The middle ages *knew* that there were other countries and other peoples beyond the bounds of Christendom, but on the whole they had little curiosity or disquiet about them. They scarcely ever thought of going to have a look at them; unlike us, they did not have an itch to push half-open doors or to go where nobody had been before. When, for example, we read in Joinville, about the exotic spices imported into Egypt down the muddy waters of the Nile, that 'These things are said to come from the Earthly Paradise', we are surprised that this thirteenth-century knight was not stirred to make further inquiries, or even to go and see for himself. And it was like that from one end to the other.

More still, these men seem to us to have been little disturbed about the ultimate fate of 'the others'; the fact has been studied in the case of St Bernard of Clairvaux, a sensitive and high-souled man if ever there was one. How is this to be explained? No doubt the conspicuousness of the Church and her far-flung triumph were so great in those days that it weakened the vigour of the consciousness one could have of what lay outside Christendom. This consciousness did not, so to say, influence ideas or the theological aspect of questions. The erring conscience had already been analysed and a theory of implicit faith elaborated with a thoroughness that has hardly been surpassed—but neither was applied to our problem.

No Salvation Outside the Church?

A change came when, after the great geographical discoveries at the end of the fifteenth and the beginning of the sixteenth centuries, Christian missionaries, principally members of the Society of Jesus, made one anthropological discovery after another of hitherto unknown peoples who were civilized *and good*. This meant eventually that the theological aspect of the problems was affected. It has been very appositely remarked that, as between the Jansenists, tied to the text of St Augustine, the doctor of predestination and grace, and the Jesuits, of whom a good number knew the Indies, China and Japan, the difference was one of ignorance or knowledge of non-Christian peoples. Here it matters little that the Jesuits at first yielded to a perhaps too easy optimism and the attractions of 'concordism',[1] which led them to find the mysteries of the Christian faith in the beliefs of the Chinese and Japanese. Little by little, new considerations made themselves felt. People's thinking had already undergone considerable development when, at the end of the eighteenth century and the beginning of the nineteenth, they realized that they were faced by a new situation in the old Christian lands themselves: whole populations that had professed Protestantism for several generations and had long known no other form of religion; an ignorance of Christianity widely spread in some sections of society; and the growth of the ideas of tolerance towards persons and of the rights due to the individual conscience, ideas which marked the eighteenth century. The influence of this last factor on the minds of Catholics cannot be overlooked.

It is a fact that from Pope Pius IX onwards the consideration of 'in good faith', which was made in catechisms from the

---

[1] *Concordism*: an over-simplified pursuit of point-by-point agreement between certain biblical data, taken materially and literally, and the statements of science accepted at a given moment; for example, between the 'days' of creation given in Genesis and the geological periods.

seventeenth century, expressly finds its place in papal documents, as the complement of the popes' very strong and very necessary condemnations of religious 'indifferentism'.[1]

Catholic theology has kept the formula 'Outside the Church . . .', but it must be recognized that it is now given a sense very different from that of its originators, Origen and St Cyprian. We shall see what that is. Briefly, it is no longer a question of applying the formula to any concrete person whatever, but of stating objectively that the Church of Christ is commissioned and qualified to carry salvation, brought by Jesus Christ, to *all* men; and that she alone, as Christ's Church, is so commissioned and qualified. So the formula is no longer to be regarded as answering the question '*Who* will be saved?' but as answering the question '*What* is it that is commissioned to discharge the ministry of salvation?'

THE CHURCH LEARNS FROM FACTS

Before going on to fuller explanations, we may draw a lesson of general significance from the history so summarily digested above.

The Church learns through contact with facts. Her understanding of her mission and what she is for men has increased in the measure that she has gained in consciousness of certain 'dimensions' of mankind and of the world. Truth remains unaltered; but it is grasped in a new and undoubtedly more adequate way when men and the world are known *as they are*, in an extent, age and goodness other than what has been believed of them before. At bottom, intellectual advance consists to a large extent in going on from words to experience, from learning and repeating formulas to personally tested conclusions, in a word, from fancies to realities. A book could

---

[1] *Indifferentism*: roughly, the attitude of mind expressed in the common phrases 'One religion is as good as another' and 'It does not matter what you believe so long as you behave well.' [*Trans.*]

be filled with examples and historical references. This is obviously a matter of great importance; but it is enough to remark here that, where mission and pastoral affairs are concerned (and even, in part, social and moral teaching), knowledge of the world and of humankind in their length, breadth and depth has a powerful influence on our access to a truth which, from being too simplified and perhaps a little childish, has to become fully informed and adult. Is not this the experience of very many apostolic men in missions in distant lands and at home, as well as in relations with Christians of other communions?

John of Joinville did not feel the urge to go and see for himself, though he was a man of remarkable 'awareness'; but we have done so, and shall not forget our experience in a hurry: every time that we have been to look we have learnt something. And even a great deal!

II   THE SALVATION OF THE 'NON-EVANGELIZED'

One of the characteristics of the present religious situation is that lay people ask difficult questions of which even elementary treatment presupposes basic knowledge that the questioners have not got. These questions do not come only, or even principally, from a minority of really cavilling Christians; they are often put by people on the edge of Christian practice, or of faith itself. That is the case with the question we are considering, the one which is probably the most common among those concerned with topics that 'give scandal': what is to be thought of the saying 'Outside the Church, no salvation'? More precisely, what are the possibilities for salvation of the 'non-evangelized'?

The question is complex. Some points are certain and held by everybody; there are others of which the explanations are disputed. Here we will try to keep as closely as possible to the most common principles.

THERE WILL BE A UNIVERSAL JUDGEMENT

In the evening of the world, that is, in the evening of his life for each individual, we shall be judged, and judged on what we have done during our bodily life (2 Cor. v. 10). Nothing is better attested by holy Scripture than this certain truth: God is just, and will render to each one according to his deeds. The texts are so numerous that we will give only the references: Psalm lxi. 13; Job xxxiv. 11; Matt. xvi. 27 (cf. xiii. 39, xxv. 19 ff.); Luke xiv. 14; Rom. ii. 6, 12–16 (read this!); 1 Cor. iii. 8, iv. 5; 2 Cor. v. 10, xi. 15; Eph. vi. 8; 1 Pet. i. 17; Apoc. ii. 23, xx. 12, xxii. 12 (cf. xiv. 15); Gal. vi. 7–9; 2 Tim. iv. 14.

We must follow up this unquestionable truth and search out its consequences. Life in the body, in time, on this earth, is the time for choice. Our freedom is not worth much if choice be considered as being determined by such or such a thing, for we are then submitting as often as we are choosing; but our freedom is real if choice be considered as the total meaning we give to the whole fact of our existence. Each of us, then, directs his heart in a certain way through the generality of his days, and all is recorded in the Book of Life. At the end, the judgement of Truth will assess the result more surely than any electronic computer: an accounting that will consist not only in the quantitative sum of our deeds, but also and much more in the bringing out of their *significance* in regard to God, his purpose and his will.

The time for choice will then have gone by, there will be no more 'in between' but only life or death (save when life, awarded at the judgement, is deferred for a time of necessary purification). Here is a consequence of the utmost importance: the good or evil of our earthly lives are good or evil in relation to *man's supernatural destiny*, in Christ: they will result in life or death for ever. There could be only three ways of avoiding this, of which two are impossible and the third extremely unlikely. The first is by the negation of it. The second is by transmigration of souls (metempsychosis), giving a man a further chance when he has not made a clear choice for, or against, God; there is no support whatever for this hypothesis, and it is contradicted by holy Scripture (see Appendix I). The third is the theory propounded by Cardinal Louis Billot in 1919–23: according to this, the great majority of people, having been incapable of a true spiritual choice, would be given a natural destiny, in that Limbo of which, it must be admitted, holy Scripture never speaks. . . .

A universal judgement that decrees life or death means that there is a universal and real possibility of eternal salvation. Reward according to one's works, bringing life in Christ or unending death, means that every person's life achieves a deep total significance which, according to the form of the choices that decide this significance, has a meaning in relation to God—the true, the living God, the God of Abraham and of Moses and of Jesus Christ.

This is what St Thomas Aquinas was driving at in a well-known text, fearlessly, quietly and laconically: 'When a man arrives (morally) at the age of reason, the first thing to which his mind must turn is to deliberate about himself. And if he directs himself towards the true end, grace is given him and original sin is remitted' (*Sum. theol.*, I–II, q. 89, a. 6; cf. q. 109, a. 3). Doubtless our present idea of personality, and our knowledge of psychological and moral life as a continuous flux, will lead us to see this arrival at the age of reason and deliberation about oneself as consisting, not so much in a single explicit act, as in a progressive unfolding of our deepest attitude towards self, others, life, the moral and spiritual Absolute. Analysed in this sense, the bearing of the passage remains the same; it is in every way decisive.

STAGES IN ATTAINING SAVING FAITH

If 'Outside the Church, no salvation' had to be taken as

excluding from salvation all those *actual persons* who do not
effectively belong to the Catholic Church, the question of final
salvation would be covered by that of knowing who is a
member of the Church. But to say that this interpretation of
the formula is not binding is an understatement: it is in fact
excluded, and excluded officially. This was seen at its clearest
when, in 1953, an American Jesuit, Father Leonard Feeney,
was excommunicated by Rome because he pertinaciously and
publicly upheld the strict and literal interpretation of 'Outside
the Church . . .'.[1] Thus a man who held, against the Church,
that all those who are in fact outside the Church are debarred
from salvation, finished up by being himself excluded from the
Church for doing so: an odd situation!

The important letter addressed to Cardinal Cushing by the
Holy Office in 1949, referred to in our footnote, will be mentioned again later. It makes reference to Pope Pius XII's
encyclical letter on Christ's mystical Body (1943), which contains some decisive explanations. There are spoken of as
'members of the Church' only those who belong effectively
to her through baptism and communion with their bishops in
union with the Apostolic See. As for those who, while not
belonging to her, do not lack 'justness', and therefore have
supernatural faith and charity and are entered on the way of
salvation, the pope refers to them as 'related to the mystical
Body of the Redeemer'.[2] In the form of moral 'justness' and

[1] This, in brief, was what happened. In 1949 the rector of Boston College
dismissed three of his lay teachers for maintaining that all those who are
not expressly members of the Catholic Church will be damned. Father
Feeney, who since 1942 had been in charge of the centre for Catholic
students at Harvard University, publicly defended the three men; he would
not desist, and for this reason, after various warnings and penalties, he was
excommunicated on 13 February 1953. This sad business produced one
happy effect: the Holy Office in Rome sent a letter to the archbishop of
Boston, Cardinal Cushing, which was a 'statement of reasons', equivalently,
a statement of the Church's teaching on this matter. The letter was dated
8 August 1949, but was made public only in 1952; a French translation of
its text appeared in *Documentation catholique*, 2 October 1952, *cc.* 1395–8.

[2] *Mystici Corporis Christi* (C.T.S. trans., London, 1944), para. 102.

divine grace, such people have dispositions which can make them Christ's saved ones, members of his Body; but they do not belong effectively to that Body inasmuch as it is visible and recognizable on this earth, that is, identical with the Church. They are indeed in line with the life of the mystical Body, but they are not—yet—effectively within its visible unity.

This teaching suggests a closer consideration of the stages of our incorporation in Christ. In a general way, the present religious situation also inclines us to consider what may be called the manifestation in time of the process of our union with him. Amongst others, Father P. A. Liégé has done this in various studies, in which he makes a very instructive distinction between the following levels in the Church, to which the duties of the ministry have to correspond: instructional community, community of faith, eucharistic community, and then, on the other side of the veil, community of glory. We are no longer living in Christendom, that is, in a unanimously Catholic society, in which one was 'of the Church' wholly and at once. Today, society is made up of numerous unbelievers (of whom many indeed are good men, and some are feeling their way towards faith), of a very large number of the indifferent or non-practising, even amongst the baptized, and of several other moral and religious worlds in addition to the Catholic one. So adherence to Christ cannot now be looked at in any simple, 'monolithic' fashion. When faced by implicit Christianity, states of preparation, progress in the right direction but its object not yet fully attained, we shall have more and more to look on them as moments of faith before Faith. Very many pastoral problems are found at these earlier stages, for so many of the people we have to deal with are not the fully practising and declared Catholics who made up so big a proportion in earlier times. At any rate in those days no attention was paid to those who were not convinced.

We are not left without help in these problems, at the level of great principles anyway, for the gospels, especially St John's, offer a fine and exact picture of the path that leads to faith, to Christ, to the kingdom of God. We have only to recall the principal elements.

THE GOSPELS TELL OF FAITH BEFORE FAITH AND GRACE BEFORE GRACE

The first three gospels report many parables and relate a number of miracles. The fourth gospel has more doctrinal discourses than parables; but it is full of actual deeds that are also meaningful, and it contains a whole theology of coming to faith through the 'signs' that Jesus gives, through the sign that he himself *is*. This fourth gospel is especially dramatic. From beginning to end there is the question whether Jesus will be received or rejected, whether darkness or light will prevail.[1] Light is proffered in such a way that a man would be blameworthy did he not see it, for it is clear enough to prescribe a duty at least to pay attention to it; but it is not so clear and certain as to be coercive, and those who refuse it can give reasons for doing so. It is not the pure objective evidence that decides, though that is enough to make faith reasonable; it is the heart, in Pascal's sense of the word, which is so close to the biblical sense: not sentiment, but the inmost disposition of the consciousness and of the person as a whole.[2]

[1] The Apocalypse shows the same drama being worked out in the life of the Church.

[2] Three great Christian geniuses, who fundamentally 'belong to the same family', give a fine synthesis corresponding to the division of minds into submissive and rebellious: (1) St Augustine, in *The City of God*, bk. xiv, ch. 28, 'The two loves'. (2) Pascal. J. Malègue's novel *Augustin ou le Maître est là* well illustrates the profound analysis of acceptance or refusal of faith. A representative text: 'It was not right that Jesus Christ should come in a manifestly divine way that would be fully convincing to everybody; nor was it right that he should come in so hidden a way that he could not be known by those who should seek him with their whole heart. To them he willed to make himself perfectly recognizable. And so, willing to appear openly to those who seek him wholeheartedly . . ., he so accommodated knowledge of himself that he gave signs of himself that can be seen by those

As an example we draw attention to the miraculous sign of the healing of the man born blind, related in detail in John, ch. 9. The re-reading of this chapter is indispensable for seeing, by an actual illustration, what we have here been able only to indicate lightly.

St John likes to speak of 'signs'. The sign is something met in life, but something that stands out amidst the multitude of other things; it is sometimes very striking, sometimes less so, and a given sign can even be, in its material aspect, something quite commonplace. The healing of a man blind from birth without the use of medical means is certainly extraordinary. But when Jesus drew Nathanael to himself simply by saying 'I saw thee when thou wast under the fig-tree, before Philip called thee', the fact can be given a natural explanation if one wishes to do so. But Nathanael immediately saw in it both the messiahship of Jesus and a call to follow him. For the most important characteristic of a sign is its ability to be *significant* for somebody who meets it and sees its meaning. In this respect, anything extraordinary in the sign itself matters but little: what does matter is its meaningfulness, that I see something in it. That presupposes that my consciousness is wide awake, or at any rate has its eyes open. My dispositions enter into the reading of the sign for what it is meant to be.

A simple illustration. This morning Helen is all dressed up. There is nothing remarkable in that. But, if Andrew is a bit sweet on her, those clothes will say something to him. If he is not, they will not, and Helen will not dress up for him again.

who seek him but not by those who do not seek him. There is enough light for those whose only desire is to see, and enough darkness for those who are not so disposed' (*Pensées*, no. 430). (3) Newman, struck by the extension of unbelief which was beginning to appear as a collective thing, a current of history, put forward an analysis, less purely inward and personal than Pascal's, of two opposed types of men, the religious and the rationalist; for references see J. H. Walgrave, *Newman: Le développement du dogme* (Paris, 1957), pp. 162ff. Eng. trans. *Newman the Theologian*, (Chapman, England and Sheed, U.S.A., 1960). See also H. Rahner, *Servir dans l'Église: Ignace de Loyola et la genèse des Exercices* (Paris, 1959).

In the healing of the man born blind there are two different attitudes to be noticed. There is the blind man himself: he is an ignorant man, but all he says testifies to his honesty, his straightforwardness, his freedom from egotistical self-justification (one is reminded a little of Joan of Arc answering her judges); and in the end he shows the depth of his character when, in reply to Jesus' question 'Dost thou believe in the Son of God?' he says, 'Tell me who he is, Lord, so that I can believe in him.' In the same way Charles de Foucauld, in 1886, when his conversion was begun but he was not yet convinced, used to pray 'O God, if you exist, make me know you!' Then, on the other hand, there are the Jews. By that term, 'the Jews', St John in his gospel points, through Jesus' actual opponents, to the world that rejects him. Their minds are closed, they have taken up their stand; it is they who are right and nobody is going to make *them* budge. The case is decided in advance: Jesus cannot come from God, for he does not observe the Sabbath; all those who follow him are to be forbidden the synagogue. The man with perfect sight whom they saw yesterday must be a different person from the blind man they had known; he is a bad lot, and what is more he tries to give lessons to the learned!

Jesus answered them with weighty and far-reaching words. 'I have come into this world,' he said, 'so that a sentence may fall upon it, that those who are blind [i.e. those who do not claim to see, and therefore do not think themselves above being enlightened] should see, and those who see [i.e. those who claim to see] should become blind.' Then the Pharisees asked, 'Are we blind too? and Jesus replied, 'If you were blind [i.e. if you did not claim to see] you would not be guilty. It is because you protest, "We can see clearly," that you cannot be rid of your guilt.' Many other passages, and indeed the whole Gospel, declare the same thing: man is able to see or not to see; he can make use of his eyes to good purpose, or else in such a way that they are unseeing. That is the meaning of the words of Isaias (vi. 9–10), often referred to in the Bible: '. . . they cannot see with those eyes, hear with those ears, understand with that heart, and turn back to me and win healing.'[1]

Parables serve an analogous purpose to that of signs. Think, for example, of the parable of the wise and foolish virgins, of the great supper, of the prodigal son: 'There was a certain man who had two sons . . .', and, no less, of the shattering tale with which the prophet Nathan brought home the baseness of his sin to King David (2 Kings xii. 1–6). A parable makes use of some simple topic, some familiar happening from everyday life: guests who refuse an invitation, a rich man who victimizes a poor man, and so on. All quite ordinary. But the thing is held up as a mirror for us to see ourselves in it, that we may learn where we stand in relation to the transcendent and undeniable truth which ought to rule our lives. A parable too has meaning for him who is ready to understand it. When Nathan told David about the rich man who seized the poor man's one lamb to make a meal for a friend, the prophet was showing David that *he* was that rich man. For he had taken the wife of Urias and, to cover his crime, had tricked her husband into going to his death. When Jesus tells the parable of the great supper (Luke xiv. 15–24), I suddenly realize that I in fact refuse inward invitations to share a bounty, and that *I* am the man who makes those excuses for doing so! The Lord has spoken to *me*.

And I, too, can put off drawing the conclusions till another time; I can turn a deaf ear, 'amuse myself', think about something else; I can take good care not to look into my own soul. That was what the Samaritan woman instinctively tried to do (John iv. 4–26), and each time Jesus brought her back to

[1] See Matt. xiii. 11; Mark iv. 11; Luke viii. 10; John xii. 40; Acts xxviii. 26–27; cf. Rom. ix. 10–18, xi. 6–8; Matt. xiii. 10–17.

herself and to the meaning of his encounter with her. He did not bring her back to an egotistical self and an easy compliance with momentary desires—that also is merely 'amusing oneself'; no, he recalled her to a reflective and attentive self, able to receive the visit of One who was appealing to her to go beyond herself. The world of today specializes in distracting men's attention: it attracts them, overwhelms them and gratifies them, all at the same time. In its insidious way, it is as effective as an H-bomb in atomizing, volatilizing and dispersing in smoke that living image of God that awaits the Spirit's call in each one of us.

So the inner disposition of the man confronted by parables or signs has a decisive influence: according to the direction in which it is turned, it enables him to grasp their significance for his life, or prevents him from doing so. It is at this very point that the gospel usage of parables and signs for the disclosing of Christ and the approach to faith can shed light on the question of the salvation of the non-evangelized.

In the Gospel, faith in Christ clearly seen and recognized comes about (or is refused) at the end of a process that begins with the appearance of a sign or a parable, and goes on with a progressive approach (or withdrawal) of Truth towards a person and of the person towards Truth; this happens in a half-light, which is sufficient for people of good will, while to others it provides the occasion and justification for their turning away. We are not examining the psychology of the approach to faith for its own sake, so we will not analyse in detail the attitudes of openness and of refusal. The gospels supply valuable information on this matter. The refusal by the 'Jews' —in St John's sense of the word—always appears as a refusal to go any farther, a refusal to re-examine accepted, well-tried, established positions. 'It is known . . . , it is settled . . .' Openness to, acceptance of, the Good News, is, on the other hand, a positive response to an invitation to 'come out of oneself'. It is always a matter of choosing something—more exactly, someone—in preference to the egotistical self (see above, note 2, p. 104).

The important thing for us is to see that final, open faith, giving its response to the plainly seen truth about Christ, is the conclusion of a movement of mutual approach between Truth and consciousness. During this process, faith (or its refusal) is gradually brought about, through attitudes which are, psychologically and morally, already anticipations of faith, and also of love and charity. We know that, most commonly, holy Scripture does not separate love from faith, but simply speaks of a living faith that includes charity. That is the more easily understood in that, at the level of anticipation or preformation, the attitude in which faith is anticipated is fundamentally the same as that in which charity is antici-pated: it is a matter of getting out of oneself, of breaking the fetters of that corrupt instinct which makes us seek our own advantage and vindication, which refers and subordinates everything to self, even at the expense of others, and ignores everything that is beyond and above *me*. Charity, says St Paul, 'does not claim its own rights' (1 Cor. xiii. 5). Christian tradi-tion sees the great line of spiritual cleavage between men in that way; St Augustine wrote in *The City of God* (bk. xiv, ch. 28): 'Two loves have made two cities: self-love in contempt of God made an earthly city; love of God in contempt of self made the heavenly city.'

Now what is to be noticed is that the preformations of faith and charity take shape in us through choices made respecting a truth—of God and Jesus Christ—which is still veiled, pre-senting itself, not *in itself*, but in other forms and under other names. When Jesus again met the man born blind, and asked him straight out, 'Dost thou believe in the Son of God?' he was addressing someone who already believed in him virtu-ally, implicitly, although the man did not know him and had not realized who he was. Faith was formed in him, in his inner response to the sign given and to Him who, whilst as yet hidden, signified his coming in that sign. If the blind man had died before Jesus met him the second time, would he not have been numbered among the saved, even though he had not expressly recognized his Saviour?

So there is an implicit faith: not exactly in the sense that medieval Scholasticism talked so much about, namely, of a *logical* implicitness, when a truth or an idea that is not recognized is contained in another that is already held; but rather in the sense of a *real* implicitness, analogous to what is hidden in every living seed. Theology speaks of *initium fidei*, faith in its initial state, and requires God's help for it, for this movement, if it be carried on, leads to faith, to perfected charity, to 'justification', and so to salvation and life without end: the Holy Spirit is at work in this from the beginning, for it is the beginning of 'a spring of water within, that flows continually to bring everlasting life' (John iv. 14).

Writing of this kind of pre-church, a church before the Church and on her threshold, formed by a beginning of faith, St Augustine refers to the case of the centurion Cornelius before his baptism, and goes on: 'in this way there come about inchoations of faith, which can be compared with the conception of a child; but to reach eternal life it is not enough to be conceived, one has to be born . . .'. And it is through baptism that we are born in that birth which makes us citizens of God's kingdom (cf. John iii. 5).

GOD'S GIFT OF CHRIST AND THE CHURCH

There is, then, a gestation in the life of a child of God, which reaches its term when we are born into God's world in the Body of Christ, by baptism and all that life in the Church to which baptism admits us. We must not, however, undervalue God's gift to us, and the realities of his positive design of grace, on the ground that ignorance of Christ and his Church does not destroy all possibility of salvation. We must learn to look at faith in the only way that is adequate to what it is. What is baptism, what is the eucharist, to bodily eyes or in the eyes of society (which depends so much on appearances or on falsehoods!) ? Mere ceremonies or touching observances . . ., empty compliance with custom . . ., things that bring good luck. . . . But to the eyes of faith they are things that *God does*; and through them, far beyond any design of our moral intentions in his regard, he himself puts us spiritually, and enables us to live, in the Body of his well-beloved Son, which is humbled on earth but is promised glory above. The soul occupies the human body only whilst that body is existing in a certain state of integrity, and in a similar way the Spirit of God, which makes us fully his children, resides only in the Church, wherein all the elements of Christ's Body exist. Outside the Church, there is action of the Holy Spirit, but he is not given himself, in person; outside the Church, there are the gifts of righteousness and of life dedicated to salvation, but there is not the fullness of the good things of the Covenant—divine sonship, real incorporation in Christ, the Holy Spirit dwelling in us.[1]

In the Church—if one is truly in her, if one is truly of her—a man not only has the promise of salvation: he lives a saved life, he lives in the kingdom of God and in fellowship with the saints (cf. Col. i. 12). The Church, on earth, is the place in which and the means by which Creation is given its full meaning. 'The world' does not trouble about her; its interest in the Church is confined to her least interesting aspects, those which still have some meaning for 'the world'—her 'magnificent ceremonies', her human power. But 'to the eyes of the heart, which see wisdom', it is altogether different: for them it

[1] See Y. Congar, *Mystère du Temple* (Paris, 1958), Appendix III (English version in preparation).

is a matter of seeing and welcoming God's purpose, his gift.

We have seen that that is the sense in which 'Outside the Church, no salvation' is now understood. A *wholly positive sense*, namely, that there is in the world one and only one reality that shows forth the gift given by God for the world's salvation, destining it to life in fellowship with him: that gift is Jesus Christ, foretold by the prophets, suffering death and rising again for us, master of truth, who entrusted to the Church, his Bride and his Body, the treasure of the saving word and the saving sacraments.

The Church here below, born of the Cross and of Pentecost, is not the Kingdom in its fullness, but its seed and beginning: her specific principle of existence is the principle of the Kingdom itself, the Spirit of Jesus, but given in faith and possessed only as an earnest, a pledge (Eph. i. 13–14; 2 Cor. i. 22; Rom. viii. 14–27). From the beginning the Church was made in order that all men and all that is in man should be united with Jesus Christ. In this sense, she is *the one* mediation of salvation for every creature who is called to it (Mark xvi. 15); the same Inspiration through which she exists inspires her universal mission. Those people who walk in the way of salvation through an encounter with God of which the Church was not corporeally the minister, those who are at any rate 'related to the mystical Body', such are not strangers to her. They are destined to overtake her at the end, when she herself will become the Community in glory and the perfected Kingdom, but in this world they are destined to her and she is destined to them. Spiritually, they exist by the Spirit which is her principle of existence; the Spirit, dominating time as well as space, hiddenly moves them towards the Church; and the Spirit impels the Church to conceive them by intention and fervency, and to carry them in the womb of her prayer, her zeal and her bride's faithfulness, she who is wholly open to and at the service of the will—over her, in her and through her—of her Bridegroom, the Saviour of the world.

Everything that is being thus prepared on earth will be accomplished eschatologically [1] when all that has been begotten during history's long ages of childbearing shall have reached its conclusion (cf. Rom. viii. 22). This will be the time when all will be made clear, 'Quidquid latet apparebit': the Church's intention and desire to include all God's children, and the hidden intention and desire of all men of good will to enter into the Covenant of Christ's Body—these will come together, they will be disclosed to one another, they will recognize and embrace one another, as Ananias recognized Paul and Paul recognized Ananias, as Peter recognized Cornelius and Cornelius recognized Peter (Acts ix. 10–17, x. 1–33).

HOW CAN CHRIST BE RECOGNIZED AND CHOSEN WITHOUT KNOWING IT?

A twelfth-century theologian, Hugh of Saint-Victor, wrote:

> There are three ways by which people can be true members of Christ: at the levels of predestination, of personal dispositions and of an effective incorporation. The first way appertains to God, who orders one to eternal life; the second is when a heathen or a bad Christian repents sincerely and walks in the path of truth and love; the third is when one submits to the Church's sacraments, the heathen to baptism, the Christian to priestly absolution. The first happens by act of God alone, the second by using our freedom, the third by priestly ministration. [2]

This theologian's aim was clearly to distinguish the elements and causes of supernatural destiny in no matter what indivi-

---

[1] *Eschatology, eschatologically* (Gk. *eschaton*, last thing): pertaining to what the Bible tells us about the end of the world. This end is not simply a conclusion, the last paragraph of history; it is the meaning of history, which keeps it going and gives it all its deepest significance.

[2] *De potestate ligandi et solvendi*, 20 (P.L. 176, 1172).

dual person. But his analysis can be applied to the categories of men at each stage of the great saving process.

We leave on one side, or rather we assume to be acquired, the first moment, that of divine predestination, which is outside our knowledge as well as our decision—though a whole school of Catholic theology thinks that predestination includes prevision of this. The second moment is that of the heathen or the bad Christian who is undergoing the hard process of being converted in the moral, and not the confessional sense of the word, which means to order his life well and uprightly. From the point of view of ideas or conscious reflections, this can come about in a great variety of ways: even for the bad Christian, who by definition knows Jesus Christ (does he?) it may happen through some duty of his state of life, or an opportunity for making an unselfish choice, or because of meeting somebody, or on hearing a sermon, or through being struck by a good example, and so on. Hugh of Saint-Victor was thinking of a heathen who encounters the Gospel. But what we nowadays know of the world, and not only of the distant lands of the Far East but of parts of our own country, and of our own neighbourhood in it, compels us to think not only of a pagan; we also think of someone baptized as a baby and given religious instruction for years as a child, who after leaving school hears nothing of Christianity, does not practise it, and eventually forgets it altogether. After puberty, all his real life speaks to him of very different things. Is not he one of the non-evangelized too? . . . The third stage is that of baptism and of confession, the stage of the Church's sacraments by which incorporation in Christ and entry into his Kingdom are fulfilled. This can be omitted here.

If the content of faith be offered in its fullness, it most certainly puts a very serious responsibility on him to whom it is offered. 'Go out all over the world and preach the gospel to the whole of creation; he who believes and is baptized will be saved; he who refuses belief will be condemned' (Mark xvi. 15–16). If Christ be proclaimed, and in the measure that he is proclaimed, it would be blameworthy not to acknowledge him: 'If I had not come and given them my message, they would not have been in fault; as it is, their fault can find no excuse. . . . If I had not done what no one else ever did in their midst . . .' (John xv. 22, 24). There is something extremely alarming in the word that brings the Good News to us. It is rather like the Law: it eventually makes a transgressor of him who, before hearing it, was in ignorance (cf. Rom. vii. 7–13). The word pronounces judgement, or at any rate it presents a fact to those that hear it, and according to their attitude to that fact the hearers go to the right hand or to the left, they become sheep or goats. And yet the message *must* be delivered. What went before leads up to it, it is a condition of the glory that God wants to receive from his free creatures. Jesus himself was seeking to bring over those to whom he offered a sign or a parable or a testimony, when he said, for instance, to the Samaritan woman, 'I, who speak to thee, am the Christ', and to the man born blind, 'He is one whom thou hast seen. It is he who is speaking to thee.'

But what does it mean, fully to set forth the Gospel? Does a completely *objective* account of it convey all the explicitness, fullness and effectiveness of the message? Is a bare declaration of what is true sufficient to make a real proclamation and presentation of that truth? If the answer be Yes, then the *Requerimiento* of the Spanish conquerors in Mexico and South America was a full presentation of the Gospel. This *Requerimiento* is by itself illustration enough of the gulf that lies between the purely objective ethical world of the past and the ethical world of today, which refuses to utter the formula 'Outside the Church . . .' without including a reference to the concrete possibilities of salvation for the moral human individual and, consequently, of his good faith—a refusal voiced by theologians since the sixteenth century, by catechisms since the seventeenth, and by the popes since the middle of the nineteenth.

The *Requerimiento*, devised by the navigator Martin Fernandez de Enciso in 1513, consisted in the solemn reading to the Indians of a manifesto, written in Spanish or Latin, which set forth a brief history of the world since its creation, followed by an account of the institution of the papacy, and concluding with the grant, by the too well-known Pope Alexander VI, to the kings of Spain of certain islands and *tierra firma*. The Indians were then required (1) to recognize the Church 'as sovereign and mistress of the whole world, the high-priest called the Pope and, in his name and place, the King and Queen Joanna, in virtue of the said grant'; (2) to allow themselves to be taught the Christian religion. If the Indians did not submit, their masters had the right to reduce them to slavery as idolaters, to take away their property and to treat them as badly as possible—it would all be their own fault. This frightful theology was enforced with whips and weapons.

Nowadays we have become so aware of the opposite aspect of the matter that we have rather to remind ourselves of the need to be concerned about truth, to recognize and respect it. But we are better informed about what constitutes *being able* to hear and understand; we willingly gloss our Lord's words as 'He who, *having understood or being able to understand*, refuses belief will be condemned'. Nor are we wrong to include in the idea of a sufficient presentation of the Gospel a consideration of men's subjective possibilities. We do not look only at those which are psychological and moral—questions of words used, attention given, and so on; we look as well at those which are historical and social. We know that social pressure, the weight of inherited prejudices, *esprit de corps*, collective complexes are all strong influences for altering the conditions in which the presentation of a message can be considered real, effective and sufficient (at least statistically, for there is always the individual exception to be remembered).

In any hypothesis, there is still the huge mass of those whom no Christian message reaches. And also all those whom the message reaches, but under a false guise: the figure of God-the-policeman, of the pseudo-marvellous, of the sickly-sentimental, and the other things that only make a grown-up man vomit. An example occurs to me from an inquiry I made amongst the children of a certain district in Paris: What idea had they got of Christmas? One of them replied, 'Christmas? Why, that's the time for pennies!'

Sometimes approach to faith is as much as broken before there has been the least presentation of the Name in which alone we can be saved; at other times it is broken because the presentation is objectively or subjectively inadequate, and so it is as good as non-existent. And yet these people—who make up much the greater part of the poor human race—have been ransomed by Christ, and are known and loved by him; and they will be judged according to their works by a perfectly just God who knows what he has given them, judged in such a way that the sentence will be death or life, damnation or salvation. We have seen that this implies that their works express an inward choice made, *really* made, at this level.

What are we going to say to that?

We will say what theology has said more or less clearly for a long time, if not always, which a dozen years ago was confirmed by the important Roman document which we have already mentioned in connexion with the 'Feeney affair' (see above, p. 102).

'LORD, WHEN DID WE SEE YOU . . .?'

A distinction must be made between what is necessary for salvation by the intrinsic nature of things and what is necessary by God's positive ordinance. To love God out of charity is absolutely necessary. Need one say that this is a condition for salvation?—rather is it the very substance of it. To be saved is to be able to give (that implies a grace), and then in fact to give, to one's life the true meaning that it has in God's eyes. Thus no one is able to be saved if he has not *really* got love for God in his heart, and a love for himself, for his fellow men and for the world that is conformable with his love for God.

The conditions for salvation which depend on God's positive will, and not on the intrinsic nature of things, are what may be called the historic forms of God's purpose of salvation. Under the Old Dispensation it involved being numbered among Abraham's posterity. Under the New Dispensation it involves express faith in the Gospel when it has been met, heard and understood, entrance into the Church by baptism, and the effective use of the sacraments of salvation: 'He who believes and is baptized will be saved' (Mark xvi. 16), 'You can have no life in yourselves, unless you eat the flesh of the Son of Man, and drink his blood' (John vi. 54). These things are holy; God has given them to us and wants us to make use of them so that we may draw closer to him. But in certain circumstances, namely, if it be physically impossible for us to know about or have access to them, or if there be a moral inability to know them, God is content that, failing an explicit profession (by hypothesis impossible), we shall adhere to them simply in virtue of a desire. What desire? To conform ourselves to his will. This desire is contained in love for him, and implicitly looks to all the positive elements of the divine will, even when circumstances prevent us from embracing them in actuality, or even from knowing them at all.

Perhaps this distinction is one of the meanings of those mysterious words of our Master recorded by St Luke (xii. 10) and St Matthew (xii. 32): 'There is no man who speaks a word against the Son of Man but may find forgiveness; there will be no forgiveness for the man who blasphemes against the Holy Spirit.'

After recalling this teaching to mind, the Roman document that brought the Feeney affair to its doctrinal conclusion added: 'It is not always necessary for this desire to be explicit, as it is in the case of catechumens. When someone is in invincible ignorance, God accepts an implicit desire, which is so called because it is contained in the good spiritual disposition by which a person desires to conform his will to God's will.' 'Implicit' literally means 'folded together', and so 'contained in'. If I do not know God's positive requirements for men's salvation, and if my ignorance is invincible and therefore guiltless, a *real* disposition to comply with them is contained in my general determination to obey God's will.

It still remains that God must be known and loved, and that one must intend to do his will. . . . Think of all the non-evangelized in China or Africa, of those who lived before Christ, of those in our own countries who are insufficiently evangelized, of 'the godless' in that dear land of Russia. When and how have they met God that they should be able to love him? We must get to grips with this question of the 'Christian implication'. It is one, moreover, that is raised by numerous facts and researches in contemporary pastoral work, many of which revolve around the organizing of special pastoral care [1] for those among the baptized who linger on the steps or in the porch of the Church rather than stand before the altar.

The Fathers, even the Apostles, seemed to think that the Gospel had indeed been proclaimed over all the earth. The New Testament speaks of the time before this as 'the age of ignorance'. It was also the time of God's forbearance, given to men that they might have opportunity for repentance (see

---

[1] *d'une 'pastoration'*: the word is not altogether exact; it should rather be evangelization. In this connexion one thinks in France of the Mouvement Populaire des Familles as relevant.

Rom. ii. 4, iii. 26; 2 Pet. iii. 9; cf. 1 Peter iii. 10; Acts xiv. 16, xvii. 30). St Paul even goes so far as to say that in those days God did not impute their sins to men (Rom. iii. 25).

We can no longer imagine that the Gospel has been proclaimed all over the earth; and we tend to extend the idea of God's forbearance to every situation where evangelization has not really taken effect. But we perhaps shall capture reality better if we apply to the non-evangelized, those to whom Jesus Christ has not been revealed for what he is—'I, who speak to thee, am the Christ'—what we have said about the stage of preformation of faith and love, the stage of initial faith and of love for God in its nascent state.

In the gospels, when there was personal contact with Jesus, the inward attitude of openness or of closedness, of going out from and giving oneself or of self-seeking, was brought about and manifested in response to a sign or a parable or a formal testimony. Now that the Lord is no longer present in the flesh, what can call forth this attitude which, since all will be judged and doomed by it to life or death, must in the End be *in reality* an attitude taken up towards God?

Here we enter the very wide field of encounter with God through means (mediations) which are not those of the positive history of salvation, since these are, by hypothesis, not obtained or not known. We may call it the realm of 'God in disguise': he is really met, the dialogue is really with him, but he does not call himself God and one does not know that it is he; the 'hidden encounter', as Canon J. Mouroux has happily called it.

Theology has now cleared up any misgivings about the element of unconsciousness that there can be in the supernatural implication,[1] and it is no less unanimous in envisaging the

[1] L. Martin Chauffier wrote in 1945 of his communist comrade in deportation, Roger Vaillant, that he was 'an iconoclast through a hidden love of a God whose approach he both dreaded and longed for'. M. Vaillant protested, writing to his friends: 'You know me, you have read my book.

spheres of God's 'disguises' and of a Christian implication very widely. Still, it is necessary to refer to some very general conditions in which a disguise can be *God's* and an implication a *Christian* one. Two of them are major conditions, each of which calls for careful explanation.

1. *An absolute that strikes a spark of love*

It is necessary that that in which someone is invited to encounter God without knowing it should have a certain absolute character which may be recognized and really respected as such.

But that is not enough, because whatever can be an end for us always has a certain absoluteness about it. Men pursue money or pleasure or glory or power, each as an end; they are absolutes for them, wanted unconditionally. But they are not properly transcendent absolutes, which make us come out of ourselves and give ourselves to something else; in money and the rest we seek self and self is what we find. What is needed is an absolute that goes beyond us and makes us go beyond ourselves, and therefore give ourselves. A love before charity must be a true love if it is to lead to charity; it must be a self-giving love, otherwise it cannot be charity's first matrix, its preformation or anticipation.

From what word of mine, what sign, what misleading action, what stammering utterance, what slip, by what method of interpretation whatever, can it be supposed that there is in me a love of God, or of any other god? ... If there be a problem that is alien to me, fundamentally alien, not only intellectually but physiologically alien, it seems to me that it is certainly the religious problem.' M. Vaillant was right on the plane of ideas or of conscious intentions. But the psychological standpoint is precisely the one to be avoided here. It is a question of a *real* implication contained in our choices and actions. Do not the communists themselves tell us that, by refusing to commit us to certain opinions (theirs) on the ground of not taking sides in matters which divide men from one another, the Church *in reality* gives her support to 'the forces of reaction'? What we are thinking of is something similar. There is no neutrality in the great conflict between Jesus Christ and Satan. But only God can read hearts.

Contrarily, when a man goes out of himself, when he gives himself to some good that surpasses himself, when there *really* is love, then there is the possibility of meeting, in the form of an absolute, the hidden God who wants to draw us to himself and save us. For he is at work on his side. Love that deserves the name is open to the infinite, it is self-giving, not just a sentimental show. If it looks to an absolute and transcendent good, it gives us a feeling of personal insufficiency. Surely a grace from God springs up in every love of this kind? Our Lord's words about Mary Magdalen, 'Many sins are forgiven her, because she hath loved much', can refer to her love, shown towards Christ, as the *sign* of the complete forgiveness of which she knew the reality and fullness; they can also refer to the Magdalen's love (its object not specified) as that which earned full forgiveness for her. In this second case, may it not be thought that when there is love—whatever its object, but a true selfless love, and one cannot 'love' just anything thus—there is grace from God, an initial giving in relation to life and the meaning of the world, whose complete fulfilment will be in Paradise?[1]

Addressing an audience of midwives in 1951, Pope Pius XII said, in accordance with traditional theology, that 'an act of love can suffice for an adult to obtain sanctifying grace and

[1] In technical theology we should refer not only to the doctrine of *initium fidei* (the very beginning of faith), but also to the Thomist idea that, while a man can do any good (natural) action whatever (e.g. a technical act of his profession) without a grace from God, he cannot without a divine grace do an act that is morally good involving his inward intention, and therefore in the line of justification or reprobation. As a literary illustration I quote Dostoevsky yet again: 'At the day of Judgement, God will appear and ask, "Where is the girl who sacrificed herself to an evil, consumptive step-mother and for other people's children? Where is the girl who had compassion for that drunken blackguard, her earthly father, without shrinking from his beastliness?" And he will say, "Come! I have already forgiven you once. . . . I have forgiven you once. . . . And now again your many sins are forgiven, for you have loved much." And he will forgive my Sonia. He will forgive her, I know he will forgive her' (Marmeladov, in *Crime and Punishment*).

supply for lack of baptism'; he was thinking of an act of love *for God*, but certainly admitting that God can be 'aimed at' through very inadequate representations, and even under other names than his. That is the case with men—whole peoples!—brought up in other religions, which may be monotheistic, like Islam, or wholly heathen. A German Benedictine missionary, Dom Thomas Ohm, has written a lengthy and fully documented study of love for God in non-Christian religions; his conclusion is that 'There is no heathen religion in which one cannot find any kind or vestige of love for God'. It is quite true that this love is often very feeble in comparison with a full revelation of the charity of Christ; but, this knowledge being absent, their love is a mediation supplying for that charity in formation in a soul, and on the basis of it these people can be justified and saved.

When one examines, as, for example, Father Riccardo Lombardi [1] has done, the possibilities of knowing at least the existence of God, and that he rewards justly according to our deserts, one may be surprised to find them more considerable than was expected. It is often a poor sort of knowledge, debased and sadly corrupt; but it too can supply for something better. Still, in the case of certain people who have been baptized and instructed in childhood, one may well ask whether their true choices of direction, proclaiming and pledging their love, were made in the sphere that is labelled religious, in which the words, God, Jesus Christ, salvation and the rest are used. God, Jesus Christ, the Gospel are in themselves the supreme realities which call for a total commitment of our freedom in view of an

---

[1] In *The Salvation of the Unbeliever* (London, 1956). This book is a very thorough exposition of the chief theories, strictly based on the well-known text Heb. xi. 6: 'Nobody reaches God's presence until he has learned to believe that God exists, and that he rewards those who try to find him.' It is interesting to notice that these words are written with reference to Enoch, who in the Bible represents 'man' (the meaning of the name). Cf. J. Daniélou, *Holy Pagans of the Old Testament* (Longmans, England, 1957 and Helicon Press, U.S.A., 1960).

eternal destiny. But how much is there of this for some people?
In the relations they have actually had with these supreme
realities, have they really reached the level of freedom and
love? Since their first communion, since they were grown-up,
have they once pledged their freedom and love in religious
matters with the seriousness they give to some choice of human
love, in work or politics or support of some cause?

And all the while there is the mass of men who know nothing of God, or whose knowledge is as good as nothing, who
give the word 'God' meanings that are absurd, and sometimes
repulsive. The question we have raised applies even more to
them. Their meeting with God could take place under the
form of one of those master-words that stand for a transcendent absolute to which they may have given their love,
words that are often written with a capital letter: Duty, Peace,
Justice, Brotherhood, yes, and Humanity, Progress, Welfare,
and yet others. People often give themselves to these ideals
at the cost of their own personal interests and comfort, at the
cost of themselves, and even sometimes of life. Is that not true
love? But there is one thing that is privileged to be a paradoxical sign of God, in relation to which men are able to
manifest their deepest commitment—our Neighbour. The
sacrament of our Neighbour!

It is privileged by its very nature, because our neighbour is
a person, and therefore something in regard to which one can
adopt a commensurate attitude by love;[1] because, too, meeting with a person, differently from meeting with objective
realities, is able to be significant of the person of God; and
again, because mediation through our neighbour is more likely
to remain unalloyed than that of other things we shall refer

[1] It is desirable to examine, and eventually to accept, certain proposi-
tions of a philosophy of the person. For instance, 'We have the idea of
absoluteness, but we think of a real absolute only as a person' (M. F. P.
Maine de Biran); 'Everything really conceived in the mind inevitably
comes back to the notion of person' (C. Renouvier).

to—it is less likely to be contaminated by the efforts of the Evil One. But our neighbour is privileged above all because God is actually present in him. It is right and it is necessary to speak of the 'mystery of our neighbour', and with the exact sense that the word 'mystery' has in the mouths of the Fathers, something which has a meaning beyond itself and in relation to the final reality towards which the whole history of salvation moves. Humanly, we never know exactly who it is we are meeting in the person of our neighbour. I am thinking of a Parisian priest who in old age used to tell how, about 1880, he gave hospitality to a priest from Italy; he was put in the attic. When Don Bosco—for it was he—was canonized, the old priest said, 'Had I known he was a saint he would have been given the best bedroom!' Divinely, even less do we know the true name of those we come across. Abraham entertained three travellers, and it was God whom he harboured (Gen. xviii). A man from Cyrene, Simon, was made to carry the cross of a stranger, a condemned man who was unable to carry it farther: he was the Saviour!

What was occasional under the Old Dispensation has become like a law since Jesus Christ took on our manhood. The outstanding example is in the twenty-fifth chapter of St Matthew's gospel, where our Master tells us clearly on what the last judgement will be based: 'I was hungry, and you gave me food. . . . Lord, when was it that we saw thee hungry, and fed thee? Believe me, when you did it to one of the least of *my brethren* here, you did it to me.' It is true that these words were directly addressed to people who knew Christ but did not know that it was he whom they had met in the persons of the hungry and thirsty, the ragged, the imprisoned and other human sufferers. They did not know that in keeping the second commandment they had fulfilled the first. Nevertheless there is still the recognition of a *real* implication in their actions, surpassing all implication of knowledge. We shall be judged on what we have done, not on what we have known.[1]

And then, *by becoming man, God has taken to himself brothers.*
We must perhaps see here an aspect, not yet theologically
clarified, but very real, of an idea often found among the
Greek Fathers: the idea that, by becoming man, taking an
individual human nature, Christ took on human nature as a
whole and transformed its state profoundly. One of the effects
of the redeeming Incarnation would be to have restored the
value of the human person as being significative of God, in
whose image it was originally made. What is quite commonly
called the objective Redemption, the fact that *we belong to a
saved world*, would have renewed the moral structure of the
world by giving it this possibility of meeting God in our
brethren, who have become his.

2. *Danger of the human absorbing the divine*

The other major condition for a Christian implication is
that what is divine shall not be swallowed up by what is
human. There are two forms of the danger.

The first is that our attitudes towards the ideals in question
can involve concrete conditions for us that are practically
equivalent to a denial or an exclusion of the Christian character of the spiritual implication of those attitudes. There is a
faith before Faith and a love before charity, but if they are
to be true anticipations they must already have, or at least
must not contradict, the characteristics of faith and charity.
A man can have a passion for justice which in fact betrays
justice, because it excludes certain people; or a love which

[1] The divine implication referred to is in the first place that of love for
God, really implied in a true love directed to a good and absolute object.
It is there because love is there, and love itself presupposes grace from the
God who wants all men to be saved, that is, that they should have a real
possibility of encountering a means to salvation. To what extent is a divine
implication actualized *objectively* in every human person as such and does
the means exist in virtue of this objective implication? That would require
a special study. More generally, it would be needful to inquire to what
extent the Reality is changed by the fact that we belong to a saved *world*.

betrays charity, because in practice it denies charity's universality or disinterestedness or some other essential value. Once more, it is not just any love, just any absolute, that can be a means to encountering God. Though they do not bear his name, they must reflect his face. God cannot wear a disguise of hatred or indulgent selfishness or pride.[1]

The second form of human danger to the possible divineness in created mediations is yet more formidable. For these mediations are objectively, or can become subjectively, idols. In loving Amida, the Buddhist who is invincibly ignorant of the true God is in reality honouring him: let us admit that. Let us admit too the possibility, *subject to what has been said above*, that heathens in good faith can serve God under the name of, for instance, The Sun. But what a problem! These mediations are 'religious', but objectively they are false and detestable— the Bible calls them shameful. But there are also the mediations provided by natural ideals, which in the end relate to man, for all that they are a reflection of uncreated Goodness and Wisdom: we have mentioned Duty, Peace, Justice, Brotherhood; then there are others, more human still, Humanity, Progress, Freedom, Science, Welfare; and why not Nation or Party—every reader can make his own list. There is a terrible danger that, instead of pointing to the God whom they conceal, these substitute absolutes should in fact take his place, that they should lose their malleability as signs and become idols falsely worshipped instead of God.

> Be blessed, O God, you who have delivered me from
> idols
> and made me worship you alone
> and not Isis and Osiris,
> or Justice or Progress or Truth, or Divinity or Humanity,
> or the Laws of Nature, or Art or Beauty,

[1] Since they are primary and fundamental attitudes of personality, faith and love exist in their wholeness, as attitudes, at each stage of their development.

you who have denied existence to all these things which are not, but the Void left by your absence. . . .

In terms of personal faith and fervour, where is the Christian who will not eagerly take up Claudel's *Magnificat*? But who, wanting to investigate a very real problem, will not also find his condemnations a little over-simplified?

ARE ST PAUL'S 'POWERS' MYTHOLOGICAL?

In St Paul's letters there is a rather mysterious theme which has exercised the minds of the learned during recent years. Paul speaks of 'Powers'. These are realities which appear sometimes as collective, sometimes, and more often, as personal; they are at enmity with Christ and Christians, whose principal conflict is with them: read Eph. vi. 10–18, ii. 2; cf. Rom. viii. 38. But Christ has already overcome and subdued them by his paschal triumph (Col. ii. 15; Eph. i. 21; 1 Pet. iii. 22), and he will complete his victory by putting them down utterly (1 Cor. xv. 24).

The subject of these Powers could be treated as a matter of mythical out-dated figures belonging to an age and an environment that are not ours. But this would be to treat it too abruptly. It is more worth while to try and grasp the very profound idea expressed in these texts of St Paul and others related to them; and we hope to show that the idea is a very important one for Christians who are conscious of their vocation in this twentieth century.

There are certain structures or institutions thanks to which or within which human activity is able to develop and increase. Considered as purely spiritual, our religious attitudes remain our secret; but when they are translated and incorporated into material substance they are made known to others, they multiply, they become operative: a tool gives me power, what I have created will remain when I am gone. Our religious attitudes are multiplied still farther when they are carried over and incorporated into a collective structure. Given the levers, a single mind can guide or influence a whole world; the man who is master of the nerve-centres of power can direct choices without number. When we consider how man fulfils his destiny in giving a meaning to things, to his work and to his personal, family, professional and civic life, we can estimate the possibilities opened up by this material and social structure of human activity.

Satan, the enemy of God's kingdom (Satan means 'adversary'), seeks to control these structures and institutions and to use them to prevent the world and human life from having their divine meaning. Jesus calls him 'the prince of this world' (John xii. 31, xiv. 30, xvi. 11; cf. Luke iv. 6; 1 Cor. ii. 6); St Paul calls him the 'prince whose domain is in the lower air (Eph. ii. 2), and even 'the god of this world' (2 Cor. iv. 4). The battle between darkness and light, which we have seen to be the general theme of St John's gospel, is also fought out, between Christ and the Devil, at this level of signs where choice of life's direction is made or anticipated, either towards self-giving, faith and charity, or towards self-seeking, personal renown and power, unbelief and spiritual death. The ambiguous mediations we have looked at overlap to a considerable extent the collective material structures in which our spiritual choices are multiplied; and the Powers in league with Satan work on them in a way that takes account neither of God nor man, and leads to death. Yes, indeed, the Powers are real, and both personal and collective: currents of history, world movements, great 'ideologies', which a malignant spirit kindles, stirs up, incites and tries in every way to bring under the dominion of the two great temptations: 'If you go all the way, if you defy the Law, you will be like gods . . .'; 'If you bow down before me, I will give you everything.' Temptation always comes to that.

Our Father! May your Kingdom come . . .! Do not let us

give in to temptation, and rescue us from the Evil One!

NEED FOR A MISSIONARY CHURCH AND PEOPLE

The Church's mission is as wide as the world. The Lord's
followers will never come to an end of evangelizing man where-
ever he is found, beginning with themselves. For he is a creature limitless in number, and complex: he is an animal, so
closely bound up with his body that each one will be judged by
the good and evil he has done while in the body; yet an animal
which builds up its own life, not only by creative work but by
giving life meaning, bringing it into relation with a spiritual
principle of existence. Therein lies the most specifying characteristic of the human condition. Man freely creates things,
by work, and he freely creates man, by giving his life meaning.

From the standpoint of the salvation of the non-evangelized,
we will consider the urgency of proclaiming Jesus Christ to
people so that, giving true significance to their lives through
and in him, they may enter on the paths of salvation and
praise of God.

It is sometimes asked, since there are such wide possibilities
of salvation, since after all there are substitute means to it,
what is the good of missionary enterprise? If being in good
faith does the work of faith, why try to instil faith at the price
of so much ill-requited labour?

That this question does not voice a real objection against
missionary undertakings is shown by the fact that the age in
which minds are wide open to what is called the wide solution
of the problem of salvation is also the age of greatest missionary
expansion. And moreover, it is largely thanks to the missions
that there is a better understanding of the exact bearing of
'Outside the Church, no salvation'.

Aristotle pointed out that movement is proved by moving.
Missions are posited by their own dynamism. Psychologically,
humanly, we can speak of an obsession by distant lands un-

visited, of an urge to push back boundaries: some men are particularly sensitive to this obsession and this urge—and a fine type of man they are. Biblically, religiously, we find, at the top of every page of history they have written, the words of St Paul: 'The charity of Christ presseth us'; we see, like the ripples made by a stone thrown into water, an unprecedented movement spreading, whose beginning was in Christ's Pasch and whose completion is in our Pentecost.[1] For the Apostles were pressed, impelled, not so much by *their* love for Christ as by *Christ's* love which, imparted to them, dwelt in their hearts and reinforced their devoted lives, seeking through them to be spread over the world: 'It is fire that I have come to spread over the earth' (Luke xii. 49). There is no need to look for reasons to justify love: it is in itself able to impart good.

Nevertheless it has its reasons, and is able to give them. In relation, very especially, to the theology of salvation we have set out, there are two great motives that make the task of evangelization necessary and urgent.

1. *The Glory of God.*

In the first place there is God's 'plan', on which all things depend for their existence and its accomplishment. Now the divine enterprise that set the world on its course and guides it to its end is a single thing, but in two stages—a bit like one of those rockets that we shoot off into the sky. Christ gave movement and meaning to the first creation; he set it on its axis and gave it momentum to go on to its end. God conceived it like that from the beginning, and so it can be what it ought to be only in and through Jesus Christ. God, twice, has laid the foundations, and twice it has been left to us to complete the work, like a schoolboy who has been given the aim and outline of a task and told to finish it. The world's mission is work, the Church's work is her mission.

[1] See Y. Congar, *The Mystery of the Church* (London, 1960), pp. 42–52.

The meaning of the world is Jesus Christ, and the Church is the means by which he is fully known and grasped.

Fullness exists only there where God is veritably present and active as he wishes to be. Now the term of his design is that he should take to himself a body and become a community. A Christian philosopher (truth to tell, a bit theosophist 'round the edges'), F. C. Œtinger, has observed with perception that 'The works of God aim at corporeity'. And in fact God did, in Jesus Christ, take a human body; in him, 'the whole plenitude of Deity is embodied' (Col. ii. 9), and through him God touches us physically as well as spiritually. And the result of what he thus imparts to us is the Church, the community of the faithful, which is the Body of the Son of God, spiritually and in very truth. God's purpose, and so the truth of the world, is actualized only when, after all their gropings towards Heaven (cf. Acts xvii. 27), men grasp this ladder let down to them from on high: the ladder of Christ's Body, which is the body of the Servant giving himself lovingly to all. The ladder can be climbed only by the rungs of humble and ministering love; it is always the ladder of the Cross, just the opposite of what the Devil offers men in the multiplicity and monotony of his temptations. That is what we give ourselves to by faith, the door through which we enter the Church of the blessed. Such is the true meaning of life: it is the road to Heaven; it is more than the road, it is already the beginning of Heaven.

This is to the glory of God, but also for the salvation of men, for their final happiness. Obviously we are much less sensible of God's glory than of our happiness. That is a mistake, for the two cannot be separated, or rather, they are really the same thing. God's glory is when his purpose is achieved, and that is when his creation is fulfilled. The petitions of the Lord's Prayer are linked with one another and explain one another; they refer as a whole to a single great reality which, through

God's will, our daily bread, freedom from the Evil One, is at the same time both God's kingdom and glory and our salvation and happiness.

That Jesus Christ should be known and followed, that his kingdom, which on earth is the Church, should spread, grow and be vitalized by the word and sacraments that come from him—these things not only mean a greater glory for God; they also mean a more assured and abundant salvation for men. 'I have come so that they may have life, and have it more abundantly' (John x. 10).

2. *To renew the warfare waged by the Prophets and to carry on that of the Lord himself*

We have to learn that the world is not neutral. No doubt it is in its material composition, but not as a world of human beings, that is, in the use we make of it and in the significance that, through this use, we give to our lives. We must go back to St John's standpoint, taken over into the synthesis of great Christian geniuses like St Augustine, St Ignatius Loyola and Newman;[1] we must look at the world's spiritual history as a huge drama played out between two camps, whose leaders are Jesus and Satan. Jesus fought this battle and defeated Satan: he overcame him at the temptation in the wilderness, when the Enemy urged him to use the world for man's power and glory; he overcame him in his passion, when he again acted according to the real meaning and true ways of life: was this to keep it for self, or was it to give it for love?

Nowadays we do not believe much in diabolical manifestations, though the pilgrim to Ars can see the scorched bed of a poor and holy parish-priest. . . . Let us say that amongst us it is now rare for the Devil to resort to childish tricks. On the other hand, ancient records are full of them. It can be freely

[1] Cf. p. 104, above. St John's outlook is also that of the synoptic gospels: see E. Mersch, *Le Corps mystique du Christ* (Paris, 1936), vol. i. pp. 30ff. Eng. trans. *Theology of the Mystical Body* (Herder, U.S.A., 1951).

admitted that they have been touched up and added to, and that natural phenomena were misunderstood. All the same, we can believe that there were such things when we consider that there still are such things. We have only to read the accounts of missionaries in heathen countries, lands that have not been exorcized, as ours have been, by centuries of celebration of the sacraments and an age-long history of Christian holiness. It is unquestionable that missionaries face a situation in which the Devil holds men in his horrible grip, often in ways perceptible to the senses. He degrades them in every possible fashion and maddens them with childish terrors, whereas Christ sets them free and ennobles them. It would be a good thing if some well-informed and critically-minded person would gather together the materials for this chapter of missionary life and history.

The Devil no longer exercises power over us by fetishism and sorcery. All right! But he has found more effective ways of 'possessing' people: those great collective institutions by means of which he perverts that use of the world through which men are called to give to their lives, in Christ, a sense of 'openness', of faith, of love, of brotherly fellowship and service. Satan has his allies in Money, Power, Public Opinion and its instruments, the Party, the Race, the Nation, and in Progress, Comfort, Production, and so on and so on. It certainly looks as if we too have our idolatries. . . .

All this is a very important aspect of missionary work, and it further emphasizes that this work is not confined to lands like Africa or China. The mission is co-extensive with the Church and with Christian life. It is a matter of fighting for Christ against domination by evil spirits. It is a renewal of the spirit and warfare of Elias and the prophets, against idolatry in all its forms, gross or subtle, against the Powers which pervert the meaning of the world and of life. It falls to us to oppose the bedevilment of the world's institutions, and, in the world's work which we share, to bear witness to the charity of Christ. Such warfare is the task and the responsibility of the apostolic Body, whose leaders are the bishops, and, with them, of the priests whom they ordain to assist them; it is the task of every Christian who is conscious of his responsibilities, whatever his place in the world's life, lowly or high, obscure or distinguished: there he has been put and there he has to manifest his faithfulness. We all can and we all must join in the spiritual battle—there is no room for neutrals: 'He who is not with me, is against me'; 'The man who is not against you is on your side' (Matt. xii. 30; Luke ix. 50, xi. 23).

At the first congress of young communists after the Russian revolution of 1917, Lenin was billed to address a large and expectant audience; he began by repeating one word three times: 'Learn! Learn! Learn!' Surely if a paradoxical Christian equivalent of Lenin, say St Paul or St Peter, had to address an expectant gathering of the whole Church, he might well begin with these words: 'Evangelize! Evangelize! Evangelize!'

Summary

'There is no salvation outside the Church.' We have seen that this statement makes no claim to be a judgement on the personal position of anybody, but that it means that the Church founded by Jesus Christ is in this world the only repository of the principle of salvation in its authenticity and fullness. In the warfare between the powers of Hell and God, she alone is guaranteed not to fail (cf. Matt. xvi. 17–19). She has been given us in order that, through her and in her, life may not be jeopardized but may receive its true meaning and attain its end, in God.

Those who, without fault on their part, do not belong to her, can nevertheless encounter things which are an occasion for them to express the true inwardness of their hearts; and thus they are able to receive a seed of faith and charity, in the same way that, in the Gospel, a disposition of refusal or of acceptance was produced by meeting signs and parables. The great thing is to decide whether one will seek self or give self. Those who have at least this beginning of love for God implicitly desire to do his will; they have an implicit and unconscious wish for baptism and the Church, and are in some degree 'related to the mystical Body of the Redeemer'.

An implicit desire, directed to the mystical Body, must normally lead at length to a formal meeting with the gospel message. Failing that, and except for a miracle or providential intervention such as can be found in the tenth chapter of the Acts of the Apostles (the centurion Cornelius) and in missionary history, the meeting with Jesus Christ will take place eschatologically, i.e. at the end. Many people will then come to know for the first time that face and that name which they have loved without being aware of it.

Our present study may have suffered overmuch from technicalness; and we now offer an idea, drawn by the Fathers from a biblical source, which would seem to be very important. It is concerned with Christ's going down into 'hell' and its significance for the history of salvation.[1] By this, men for whom it had been impossible to know Christ were enabled to encounter him in person and to have contact with *his redeeming body*. According to several Greek Fathers, this meeting and contact are, for those who lived before Christ and outside his Church, the moment when the disposition favourable to Christ which they had conceived is fulfilled in the presence of its object and when the equivalent of baptism becomes effective; their implicit desire for it is consummated in the Reality. Those who would have believed in Christ if

---

[1] See Rom x. 6–7; Acts ii. 24–31 (Col. i. 18); Eph. iv. 8–9, and perhaps v. 14); I Pet. iii. 18–20; Apoc. i. 18. Cf. the author's *Mystère du Temple* (note 1, above).

they had lived in gospel times and had heard the Good News are set free and fully incorporated in his Body, towards which their good will, upheld by God's grace, had disposed them.[1]

For our part, we are fond of recalling—with perhaps a certain extension of its primitive meaning—the lovely prayer that has come down to us through the most ancient anaphoras (eucharistic prayers), particularly that of the *Didache*, 'Teaching', a non-biblical writing probably contemporary with the Apostles and ante-dating some of the New Testament writings:

> As this bread that is broken was scattered upon the mountains and was gathered together and became one, so let your Church be gathered together from the ends of the earth into your kingdom: for yours is the power and the glory for ever. Amen.

> Be mindful of your Church, Lord, deliver her from all evil, perfect her in your love. Gather her, your holy Church, from the four winds into the kingdom you have prepared for her: for yours is the power and the glory for ever and ever. Amen.[2]

Here is something that actually happened in October 1955. The father of a ten-year-old boy, blind practically from birth, took the child from Brittany to Lourdes, there to pray 'Lord, give sight to my son!' During the stations of the cross, suddenly the child could see. He turned his eyes to his father and saw his face for the first time; and his first words were: 'Fine! Everybody's here!' Is that not a parable of what will happen at the end, when many people's eyes will be opened at last and they will see their Father's face? Overwhelmed by God's goodness, will they not say, 'Fine! Everybody's here!'?

What new Jerusalem,
Shining in splendour, comes out of the wilderness,
Her brow marked with a deathless mark?
Sing, peoples of the earth!

[1] Thus Clement of Alexandria and Origen, and also Ambrosiaster, St Cyril of Alexandria, St John of Damascus and Oecumenius.
[2] *Didache*, 9, 4 and 10, 5; for its date, see J. P. Audet, *La Didachè*. . . . Cf. the Anaphora of Sarapion (early fourth century).

Jerusalem is born again, more lustrous and more lovely!
  Whence come these to her on every hand,
These children she bore not in her womb?[1]

Note

In the numerous recent writings relevant to our subject,
there is to be noticed a growing development of a very interesting idea, that of the sacramentality of the Church. It had
already been outlined by Father J. V. Bainvel in his *Hors de
l'Église point du salut* (Paris, 1913), and it has now been treated
for its own sake by a German Jesuit, Father O. Semmelroth,
in *Die Kirche als Ursakrament* (Frankfurt-on-Main, 1953).
Other writers have applied it to our problem, among them
H. de Lubac, *Catholicisme* (Paris, 4th ed., 1947, pp. 192ff.;
Eng. trans. *Catholicism*, Burns Oates, England, 1949 and
Sheed, U.S.A., 1958) and *Méditations sur l'Église* (Paris, 1953,
pp. 157ff. Eng. trans. *The Splendour of the Church* (Sheed, England
and U.S.A. 1956); J. Gribomont in *Irénikon*, vol. xxii (1949),
pp. 345–67; and F. Lochet, *Fils de l'Église* (Paris, 1954, pp.
37ff., Eng. trans. *Fides*, 1956) and *passim*. It is argued that,
on the one hand, mankind is one whole and that, as one
whole, it is saved in Christ (an idea that has excellent
support in the Fathers; cf. de Lubac); and that, on the
other hand, the Church on earth is the sign, an 'efficacious
sign', that is, the sacrament, of this universal redempion. That
introduces, into the Church's presence and action (invisible as

[1] Racine, *Athalie*, iii, 7, with reference to Isa. xlix. 18–21, liv. 1–3, lx. 4
(cf. Bar. v. 5–6; Zach. ii. 8). The pattern of salvation is marked by a series
of 'goings out', of which the first, from Egypt, renewed in the second, the
return from Babylon, foreshadows Christ's 'passage' in his Pasch, and its
fruit in the final Easter of the world. Each time, but only at the last in its
definitive fullness, the truth of *salvation* is made actual: '. . . men that are
bound in darkness restoring to freedom and to the light' (Isa. xlix. 9). Only
at the end of things will that which was hidden be made plain, 'Quidquid
latet apparebit'—the 'hidden encounter' with God, and the implicit desire
for Christ and his Church which so many will have had in their hearts,
and the design of universal salvation that has always inspired the Church
(cf. Rom. viii. 18ff.).

regards its essence) in the midst of the world, a kind of universal purpose which is expressed in the missionary aspect of her whole life. In this context we can conceive more adequately the relationship to the visible Church of the aim and beginnings of salvation which move the whole of mankind. And we can do this better still, the better the meaning of 'Outside the Church . . .' (in some respects an unfortunate formula) is explained and understood. For long it was taken in a sense which excluded from salvation such and such a man or such and such a category of men, and no doubt that is how its originator, St Cyprian, understood it. For the theology and teaching authority of the Church today, it is not a declaration of the salvation or non-salvation of any man whatever, it is a principle about the Church: she is the institution to which universal salvation is committed. Certainly this means that she is the *only* such institution; but it also means that she is this effectively, and that she is able to ensure salvation for every person who does not refuse it.

III   IS ONE RELIGION AS GOOD AS ANOTHER?

Does not a wide solution of the question of the salvation of the non-evangelized come in effect to a supplying for Faith by good faith? Now our contemporaries are very much at home with good faith. They are 'all for it', and convinced that it is on their side, an ally all the more reliable because it seems to be part of their very existence.

Far be it from us to question the value of sincerity, even if the world today misuses it and almost makes a religion of it. It bears within itself a possibility of the deep harmony with the Gospel that truth requires. Among people today, it often is evidence of a healthy reaction in favour of man amidst a society that tends to dehumanize, of a quest for real fellowship which is mistaken only in so far as it stops at forms that are of minor importance, or even deceptive. It is not at all a matter of criticizing sincerity in general, but of criticizing, in the light of our previous chapter, the misuse that can be made of it. All that we have written shows that we do not underrate or misconstrue the worth of good faith—we simply want to protect it against its own myth and save it from destroying itself.

Modern man is convinced, not only of his good faith, but of the sufficiency of that good faith. He readily believes that truth and error have nothing to do with his salvation, which he sees purely as a matter of honesty of intention. He has learned from some of his prophets a *mystique* of sincerity. But he thinks of this sincerity only in relation to himself; he does not consider that it is subject to an estimate of worth and that a subjectively sincere attitude may be in fact false and ruinous. Was not Hitler sincere? Are there not people who lie wide-eyed? When some expensive professional of shamelessness, such as Dawn or June, informs her admirers of her sincerity, it can but be said that it is a destroying of what is noblest in man, for it is a destroying of human responsibility. 'I don't love him any longer,' says Dawn, 'I am taking somebody else.' Simple, isn't it? It is as much as to say that 'There is only myself in me, and it is a self reduced to its surface, to the immediate moment. I take no responsibility for what I do.' Every responsibility is a response, as the word indicates. It implies that I am not alone, that someone else has a claim on me and my doings. It is just the opposite of a *mystique* of pure sincerity in the manner of Rousseau or Gide.

This bogus mysticism, with the loss of the sense of dependence, of the response to be given to him who has a right to it, is one of the causes of the lack of the sense of sin which is so characteristic of our time. Man wraps himself up in the feeling of his own innocence, he has never failed anything or anybody; at bottom, he owes nothing, he does not feel under any obligation. Descartes reduced evidence to the consciousness of thinking, and contemporary man as it were reduces all obligation to himself and his own consciousness. Quite freely, and with an innocence that knows no need to cover himself with fig-leaves, he plucks and eats the fruit of the tree of the knowledge of good and evil, which is to say that he presumes to decide what is good and what is evil by himself, without reference to any positive commands. What it comes to is that he decides what pleases him and what displeases him.

PEOPLE ARE INTERESTED ONLY IN THEMSELVES

This reducing of all to a conscience that is not controlled by objective references is in these circumstances simply a reduction to man. Modern man is interested only in himself. He no longer conducts his life in accordance with motives from above, but in accordance with his own interests, convenience and pleasure. Chateaubriand, who was sometimes a discerning observer of the great changes he lived through, remarked that under the Empire French society exchanged a morality of duties for a morality of self-interest.

Today, people judge everything by its results *for man*. They will even welcome religion when it serves human utility: 'Sisters of Charity are all right; but what is the good of Carmelites?' If religion makes parental authority respected, helps to keep society balanced and healthy, contributes to the country's tranquillity, brings succour to the needy, then we will admit that it is a necessity. But this is to value it only because of its beneficial consequences for earthly life. And even if one goes further and maintains (as of course many people still do) a positive attitude towards religion in itself, one may still be content to appreciate its value without reference to questions of truth or exclusive legitimacy. Whether or not he has read their works, man clings to certain beliefs of his eighteenth-century teachers. Since the Encyclopedists and Kant, he believes that it is hardly possible to attain a truth that is definitely true in religious or metaphysical matters, with the exception of the moral imperatives whose source is conscience. He has not read Lessing, but he eagerly accepts the conclusion of *Nathan the Wise*. If he expresses a religious sentiment, it is that the essential thing is to climb the hill; by what path does not matter, one is as good as another, and it is best to find one for oneself.

It is not such reflections as we have made that confirm him in his notion that all religions are equally good: what matters to him is that the religion be practised. Have we not indeed recognized some want of co-ordination between *the idea* which one may have (or not have) and *the practice*, even a certain effective primacy of practice over idea? We shall not be judged on what we have known, but on what we have done: 'Not every one that saith to me, Lord, Lord. . . .'

In this connexion, there is an 'indifferentism' which seeks its confirmation in what it claims to have observed hundreds and hundreds of times—that Christians, Catholics, are no better than anybody else. To this there is added a confused recollection (confused, but none the less for ever inspiring practical conclusions) of certain historical facts—dogmatic certainty which was often stirred to intolerance, and that led to hangings and burnings, merciless torture and massacre. It would be hard to overestimate the influence that religious wars and persecutions have had in directing modern ideas towards doctrinal liberalism and religious indifference.

Popes and bishops and Catholic spokesmen have not ceased to fight this indifference, for they know from experience that no door gives an easier entrance to irreligion. It is only a step from 'One religion is as good as another' to 'No religion demands our adhesion', and from that to 'One can reject them all, and have one's own' and still keep that honesty which is their common denominator of utility. Pope John XXIII's encyclical letter *Ad Petri cathedram* (1959) again included a passage against this scourge of 'indifferentism'.

By a studious comparison of one religion with another, it can be shown that the motto of religious indifference, 'All religions are equally good', is false. The rational inquiry and analysis made by Henri Bergson led him to a conclusion in favour of the Catholicism of the saints and mystics. But we cannot pursue that path here; we have to judge indifferentism from the standpoint of our problem, salvation, and within the framework of the wide solution which is now common teaching.

INDIFFERENTISM DESTROYS GOOD FAITH

There is good faith only when one is actively open to the truth in so far as one is in a position to know it. He who maintains from the start that it is 'all the same', and that there is no need to bother about truth, is destroying in himself the very roots of good faith, for he is holding indifference to truth as a principle. He is treating truth as a stranger instead of a friend, as something unimportant instead of as the pearl of great price. He is putting himself outside his kingdom.

Good faith is not a dull unconcern about what is true, a sort of moral illiteracy masquerading as innocence. It is a plant that grows at a certain level of virtuous life, that is, of making good use of our freedom.

May we add in passing that it is the same with tolerance, which is so to say a first cousin to good faith. Tolerance is not a feeble attitude which passes anything because it is itself attached to nothing; it is the good and far-seeing attitude of a person who is so enamoured of truth that he refuses to disregard any element of it, wherever it may be found and however mixed with indubitable error. Obviously that means that he is sufficiently aware of the real state of things not to be taken in by the ridiculous fiction which assigns all the light to one side and all the darkness to the other. Intolerance generally arises from lack of culture or from over-simplification. But a recent inquiry into the religious attitudes of the 'Nouvelle

Vague' in France produced a significant result: to the question 'Can a person of another religion be saved?' 60 per cent of people from 18 to 30 years answered Yes; and of this 60 per cent, 80 per cent were convinced and practising Catholics.

Indifferentism assumes that we are alone in the world, enjoying a state of sovereign and creative freedom, ourselves conditioning our own lives, which are conditioned by nothing else, situated according to our own choice and not by anything or anybody else. What childishness! Religiously speaking, we are conditioned and put where we are by an initiative of God. We are not like some imaginary country without a neighbour or partner in the world, a kind of Utopia, inhabited by a people that has no history, which carries on its trivial, self-sufficient existence in some dream-state of innocence. Why, Robinson Crusoe himself eventually came upon a band of cannibals, from whose hands he was able to rescue Man Friday!

God does not impose himself on us—that is why we are able to behave as if we had never beheld him—but he offers man his covenant. He gives many signs of it, not plain enough to have compelling force but sufficient to call for attention. Our good faith is measured, on the one hand, by the strength of attraction of the signs of God's approach which are offered us, and on the other, by the possibilities of taking notice vouchsafed us. But if, through slackness or unconcern, our eyes wander and we cease to pay attention, we sterilize good faith at its roots. Our innocence is then no more than a dream, for we have killed it. We think ourselves whole and free, but we are not: the situation has lost its integrity.

THE DAY OF WRATH WILL COME

In a general way, every gift received, every possibility accorded, creates a corresponding obligation. Nothing is received in vain or without the duty that goes with it: 'Much will be asked of the man to whom much has been given'

(Luke xii. 48). A beast of the field has no responsibility; a man has, and it is in proportion to the gifts of consciousness and knowledge that have been given to him.

Truly enough, many people have been so poorly endowed that God will ask little of them: 'For to him that is little, mercy is granted; but the mighty shall be mightily tormented (Wis. vi. 7). All the same, I personally am frightened at the ease with which so many men—and I am thinking only of my own acquaintances and those whom I meet every day—calmly banish from their lives the thought of God and of the covenant he offers us in the Gospel of Jesus Christ, of which the Church of the saints is the sign amongst us. They just go quietly on as if the problem did not exist. The bell rings to call them together for the offering of the Sacrifice of love's covenant; they go on doing odd jobs about the house, or they take a walk, or idle about by sea or river. If they had no means of knowing, they would be like the Chinese or the Tibetans, who have never heard a word about Jesus Christ and so are blameless for not inquiring about him, who will, as St Paul says, be judged not on positive law but on that of their conscience (Rom. ii. 14). But these men whom I meet *have* the means of knowing, they *ought* to be uneasy. Or they have even known Jesus Christ, they have had a first approach from him; the covenant has been offered them. If they go on turning a deaf ear, the time during which God's patience keeps the offer open will come to an end. Instead, the day of wrath will come. The last penny will have to be paid: those who through light-mindedness or self-centredness have ignored God's message of peace, those who, as the Gospel puts it so forcibly and yet gently, have not recognized the time of Christ's visiting them (Luke xix. 44), will see the coming of the moment when, the hour for choice being passed, they will have despairingly to harvest the grapes of wrath.

There is a terrifying light-mindedness about those people

today who imagine that 'everything will be all right', at any rate the more serious things, who imagine that God is all forgiveness and no severity. Indeed it is true that God is kind, slow to anger, swift to forgive (cf. Exod. xxxiv. 6–7; Ps.cxxix. 4, 7); but it is also true that he will not tolerate our deriding him for ever, him, God the all-holy! 'He who [having understood or being able to understand] refuses belief will be condemned' (Mark xvi. 16); 'Thou, by the stubborn impenitence of thy heart, dost continue to store up retribution for thyself against the day of retribution, when God will reveal the justice of his judgements. He will award to every man what his acts have deserved . . .' (Rom. ii. 5–6). In that direct fashion of his to which love for God gave an irresistible intensity, St John Vianney said: 'The good God is not spiteful, but he is just. Do you suppose that, after you have despised him all your life, he will throw his arms round your neck?'

For every man and woman there is the possibility of being lost for ever.

This possibility must be taken with the utmost seriousness.

IV   DEAD BEFORE THE DAWN OF REASON . . .

Where is the priest who has not been asked by some stricken mother, 'Is my child not with God in Heaven because he wasn't able to be baptized in time?'

The death of little children is a most upsetting thing, a grievous ordeal for the heart, and for faith too. The problem of their eternal destiny is one of the most difficult in the whole of theology.

People nowadays are less conscious of *God's* point of view, of the gratuitousness of the salvation that he gives and of the objective conditions that he attaches to the gift, than they are of *man's* point of view, and that of the individual person. Seeing that 'it is not their fault', it seems to be impossibly harsh, if not formally unjust, if these little ones are to be excluded from the fullness of the happiness that grown-ups can hope for.

But there are other reasons why the question of these children's everlasting state has so often been a practical preoccupation of theology in recent years. The question frequently comes from the most Christian of the 'young homes'. And in these days the religious dispositions of Christians are touched by certain currents of thought which seem to offer fresh considerations for theological examination: the Church's faith, God's 'plan', the reality of Christ's universal primacy, the mystery of death. . . . But theologians have yet to reach an agreed conclusion that is wide, encouraging and consolatory.

Two preliminary remarks are necessary. (1) The question is generally brought up in relation to the death of the unbaptized children of Christian parents, but the problem goes far beyond that. It applies to all who die before the awakening of reason, that is, if they have not heard of Jesus Christ or have not been baptized in his name, before the moment when they are able to make a free moral act relating to the general direction of their life: an act, that is, on the basis of which they can be justified and saved, since they are in ignorance about the true God in good faith. It is a matter of millions of little human beings, our brothers and sisters, whose long and pitiful tale makes up what in statistical tables is called 'infant mortality', of whom a very large proportion have come into the world in places where or at a time when Christian baptism was unknown.

(2) And there is this preliminary question: What *can* be known about a problem of this kind? What is there to go on that will enable us to know anything about it? Christian feeling is a fine and holy thing; but it is not enough, it needs to be enlightened. From whence can light come? From the source of all authentic Christian knowledge, the holy Scriptures, which impart to us God's mind as it is understood in the Church's tradition. And then from Christian thought making

use of what is called the 'analogy of faith'. That means the light that is obtained from the relating of a teaching, in itself not clear, to other matters that are clearer and better understood, the agreements that can be found between such a teaching and doctrines that are certain or well supported.

There are some words of St Paul which, at first sight, seem to bear on our problem; he is writing about marriages between pagans and Christians, and after remarking that the Christian partner sanctifies the non-Christian partner he goes on: 'Were it otherwise, their offspring would be born under a stain, whereas in fact it is holy' (1 Cor. vii. 14). There can be no doubt that St Paul intends to convey that children born of parents of whom at least one is Christian are by that fact destined to be members of God's people, or even that they are already members. But he does not say a word here which bears on what happens to children who die unbaptized. To apply this text to our problem it would have to be so extended or 'interpreted' as to deprive it of all value as scriptural evidence. We can, however, find some indication in it: to be born of a Christian parent or parents has a bearing on the religious situation, it involves a certain introduction to the Covenant.

All Catholics are in agreement upon certain substantial positive points.

(1) In any case, the children of whom we are thinking are not unhappy. Even if they are excluded from the highest kind of fellowship with God, which is to see him as he sees us (1 Cor. xiii. 12), to share as sons in his inheritance of glory, they are not consigned to the pains of Hell. They do not suffer the burning agony of being inescapably bound to an existence that is without meaning, and without hope of any. They are not punished. They love God with all the love that a being who is not born again in Christ is capable of.

(2) They participate in some way in the Redemption, for

they belong to the human race which Christ ransomed as a whole. But in saying that, one is speaking of what is quite commonly called the objective redemption. It matters little whether one does or does not use those expressions, objective redemption, subjective redemption. It is enough that there should be a sense in which we are already saved, in which *all* men *are* saved, and a sense in which salvation has still to be attained by each one, for it is possible to lose it. We are saved in the sense that God's righteous anger is taken away, his justice has been satisfied. The Covenant is offered anew, it is open to us, but we have to accept and enter in. The Redemption has to be applied *to persons*. The question is to know on what title, complete or incomplete, and in what way it is applied to children.

(3) The means and conditions for the applying of the Redemption are baptism and faith: 'He who believes and is baptized will be saved; he who refuses belief will be condemned.' In baptism, Christ does *all*: it is indeed a second birth. That is why baptism can be conferred on babies, without any personal co-operation on their part. The element of faith on the human side is represented and anticipated in the godparent, in the action that he takes, jointly with the child's parents, in presenting him for baptism; that action is equivalent to an undertaking to initiate the child into faith. And when the child attains the use of reason and freedom, it is for him to honour that undertaking. Such is the normal way of salvation, bound up with the essentially apostolic or missionary institution that God has given to the world to continue the work of 'him whom God has sanctified and sent into the world' (John x. 36).

When it is *not possible* to follow this way because the Gospel has, through no moral fault on his part, not reached a man or has not been put before him sufficiently, then there is another road, which eventually joins the first: a free and fundamental directing of life that implies an act of love for God, and so an act of faith. This disposition, which really involves a will to obey God, is equivalent to a desire for baptism, even though baptism is unheard of and not concretely offered. This has already been explained.

So far, everybody is in agreement; but not further.

Both the above ways are closed to the young children we are concerned with: the first because, if born of Christian parents, they have nevertheless not been baptized, or if born of heathen parents, there is no question of baptism; the second because their mental development precludes the possibility of making any choice whatever, and so, again, there is no question of it.[1]

At least that is what most theologians say up to the present. They say that these most pitiable amongst those whom Christ has saved benefit in the Lord's work to the extent of all that a child of Adam can receive of it, short of an effective *personal* application (by the above two means). They will rise again, not to a resurrection of judgement (John v. 29), not to flames and despair, but to a life of natural happiness: not without a natural love for God, yet without the intimacy and the glory that the sons of adoption will receive in the Kingdom. This state or place is called Limbo. The word comes from the Latin *limbus*, meaning 'edge' or 'border', and the Fathers, who were the first to use the word, were thinking of something *on the verge* of Hell; it can equally well be thought of as a state 'in the margin' of the essentially christological scheme of salvation. Father Lorson has called it 'The eternal nursery', and the phrase is not so fanciful as it may appear.

However, it must be admitted that what is called Limbo does not figure, clearly or obscurely or even by way of hint,

[1] Not having made and not being able to make any *personal* act, these children come before God simply in a state that is due to their parents: either baptized, and therefore reborn in Christ, or with the original stain still on them, and therefore excluded from the fellowship of God's children.

in the biblical revelation. It is in theology rather like the planet Neptune was in astronomy between the time when Leverrier deduced its existence by calculation as being necessary to the equilibrium of the heavens and the time when Galle actually saw it at the end of his telescope, visible at the spot Leverrier had indicated. It can be said that Limbo represents a doctrine commonly taught in the Catholic Church, but that it has never been the object of a dogmatic definition.

One may ask oneself whether the prolongation of a *tertium quid* beyond the Lord's return in glory is wholly consonant with God's design as a whole as it is made known to us by the Bible. Here below, so long as history lasts and we use our freedom for better or worse in earthly time and in our bodies of flesh, there exist a Church, a World (in the bad sense) and a Cosmos which is neither Kingdom nor Anti-kingdom, but simply the neutral framework of existence and choice. But in the beyond, there should be only Kingdom and Anti-kingdom, Heaven and Hell. Is it necessary to think that children who, precisely, have not known the Cosmos as a place and time of choice (because they were incapable of choosing), should for ever belong to a sort of middle state, a No-man's-land of God's plan? Would this be in accord with what St Paul tells us about Christ's sovereignty? From the theological point of view, is not to talk of purely *natural* bliss to objectify an abstraction, necessary for analytical purposes but having no place at the existential level? And, too, there is a question, to which we very well know there is no answer forthcoming, but which is worth asking in technical theology, namely, with what body and in what state will these children rise from the grave?

The upholders of this or a similar position appeal to patristic tradition and to a number of statements by the Church's teaching authority, to which indeed very careful consideration must be given. But there are two remarks to be made:

(1) According to good theological method, these texts and evidences must be subjected to a rigorous critical examination, to ensure that they are not made to say more than they in fact do say. This examination has been made,[1] and it results in a notable lessening of the weight of these texts in their category of doctrinal norms. It remains indisputable that as a whole they are not favourable to certain attempts to solve the problem in a large sense.

(2) But these attempts are really all part of the general movement of ideas about the problems of salvation, especially of the salvation of people who are outside the regular framework of positive means and ways instituted by God. We have seen that understanding of the permanent principles of the question have changed with the change in our knowledge of the real situation of mankind.[2] Though exploration has been made in this direction, we do not think that our *present* knowledge about consciousness in the newly-born, or about death, demands that a change be made in views that can be regarded today as traditional or classical. But in this as in certain other matters we prefer to make a reservation about a possible future. The door to be kept open corresponds to the two ways of salvation that have been spoken of: the way of baptism and the way of a moral choice.

Some writers (Klee, Father Mulders) have put forward the hypothesis of the possibility of a free act, through a spiritual light given by God, just before the moment of death, or,

---

[1] See the important study by Peter Gumpel, s.j., 'Unbaptized infants: May they be saved?' in the *Downside Review*, vol. lxxii (1954), pp. 341–58, with its addition in the same review, vol. lxxiii (1955), pp. 317–46. These contain ample bibliographical references and critical reports. C. Journet in *La volonté divine salvifique sur les petits enfants* (Paris, 1958) holds the thesis of Limbo and natural happiness.

[2] In any case it is a fact that in these matters we no longer hold some patristic positions, or at least we honour the principles that led to these positions but differently from the Fathers. They did not know our idea of implicit faith. St John Chrysostom and other Fathers believed that catechumens were damned if they died before actually receiving baptism.

according to others, at the moment that follows death (Father Laurenge). In our view, this second hypothesis cannot be accepted, because we are to be rewarded according to the good or evil we have done while in the body (cf. 2 Cor. v. 10). We have seen that Mgr Glorieux suggests the very instant of death (see p. 89, above). Who would dare to say peremptorily that such an hypothesis must be altogether excluded? What do we know of the little child's consciousness that would allow us wholly to deny it the equivalent of what we know in the consciousness of the adult, of which we have experience? Certain unfortunate happenings of the past (Galileo!), the extraordinary growth of knowledge within a short space of time, ought to make us careful. It may be objected that we have nothing to go on and so no means of knowing in what terms any choice would be presented to a small child. But need this difficulty be considered insuperable and the suggested way closed?

Or again, cannot Christ, in merciful response to the faith and prayers of Christian parents and of the Church, bring about the equivalent of baptism, according to that free grace of his which falls on whom he wills? Christ, said Nicholas Kabasilas, baptizes those whom the Church does not baptize. And if the Church does not baptize them, it is not through her fault: for she wants to baptize them, and in all her life of prayer and celebration of the sacrament of redemption she never ceases to intercede for their salvation. Hers is a motherhood that is always loving and kind. She who with her faith answers for the baptism of our children, would answer in advance, through the very universality of her desire and prayer, for those invisible baptisms, if it should please the Lord to bring them about.[1] Kabasilas did not know anything

[1] 'God's Church, the loving mother of the human family, embraces with perfect charity all men of every race and kind whatever; and by her prayer and strivings helps on their salvation and true happiness' (Pius XII, *Audistis Venerabilis*, 1939).

more than we know. We are not 'laying down' anything: we are simply pointing out the unquestionable way of God's wholly unconstrained mercy. Who would dare uphold any theory whatever without allowing room for that to enter in at his good pleasure, and with that mercy, clinging wholly to it, the trusting hope of Christian parents? The fact of the martyred Perpetua's intercession for young Dinocrates (see p. 65, above) has not got the value of a doctrinal authority, but it certainly has value as an example. There is nothing to prevent its being followed, and offered to God as a kind of precedent of his mercifulness.

In his address to Italian midwives in 1951, Pope Pius XII, with all Catholic tradition behind him,[1] stressed that they must minister baptism without delay when there is danger of death. 'As things are at present,' he said, 'no other way is seen of imparting this life [of Christ] to little children.' Notice the carefulness and discretion of those words. They accurately sum up the Church's tradition, which itself interprets the Scriptures: 'No man can enter into the kingdom of God unless birth comes to him from water and from the Holy Spirit' (John iii. 5). There is only *one certainty* about the salvation of little children—and that is it. All the rest is hypothesis. But there are hypotheses that warrant a larger hope; the way is not closed to them.

[1] Amongst the Copts of Egypt, no longer in communion with Rome, who for twelve hundred years have manifested the earnestness of their Christianity under Moslem domination, baptism is ministered only three or four times a year; the babies accordingly are from three to five months old. If they die before baptism, it is assumed that they are saved and nobody worries on their account.

I I

What Do We Know About the End of the World?

WE are happy to echo Claudel's reply to the inquiry 'What do you know about God?' His answer was 'Nothing more and nothing less than the catechism tells me about him.' That is enough in the full measure that faith is enough. But the state of things confronting the Christian today requires an *instructed* faith, so that he may be able to stand up for it before anyone who may ask his reasons for the hope that is in him (1 Pet. iii. 15). And so, taking the Bible as our guide, we will look at (1) what God's word says about the end of the world; (2) the question 'When?'; (3) the signs that will go before; (4) the relationship that can be found between our present world and the world to come, the new heaven and the new earth that are promised us.

1. *The great positive and absolute declarations of God's word.*

There are three principal ones. Turn to the New Testament.

This world will come to an end. Its 'fashion' passes away: 1 Cor. vii. 31; 'heaven and earth shall pass away': Mark xiii. 31; Matt. v. 18; 2 Pet. iii. 12; Apoc. xx. 11, xxi. 1, 4; cf. Isa. li. 6.

There will be a 'day of the Lord' (2 Pet. iii. 12), which will be a *judgement* on the world, or, more exactly, on history.

Like the owner of a field, who in summer time sends

harvesters to gather the crop and to throw away or burn whatever growth is useless, so in the evening of the world God will reap his harvest (Matt. xiii. 39–43) and render to each man according to what he has done (*ib.* xvi. 27; Rom. ii. 6). There will be as it were a dissolution of *this* world (2 Pet. iii. 12), but also a rebirth of the world: Jesus calls it 'the regeneration' (Matt. xix. 28), St Peter, the restoration of all things (Acts iii. 21), St Paul, the making known of the sons of God, liberation from the tyranny of corruption, the glorious freedom of God's sons (Rom. viii. 19, 21), St John, and St Peter again, 'a new heaven and a new earth' (Apoc. xxi. 1, 5; 2 Pet. iii. 13); cf. Isa. lxv. 17, lxvi. 22).

All this is bound up with the fact of Jesus Christ, or more exactly, with our Lord's Pasch. This Pasch was death in the flesh and resurrection to incorruptible life, coming from the Spirit. But it is the Pasch *of the Lord*, not of just any man, or even of a merely superior man or of a man of God, but of someone who was both truly God and truly man, fully of this world and fully from on high. How right and how consoling it is to sing during Advent that verse from Isaias: 'You heavens, send dew from above, you skies, pour down upon us the rain we long for, him, the Just One; may he, the Saviour, spring from the closed womb of earth!' Yes; Jesus belongs both to Heaven—conceived of the Holy Spirit—and to earth, to our earth and our human race, which is as it were the living highest point of all earthly dust. Coming from the earth, he is part of the harvest; coming from Heaven, yet more—being truly God, he can but be ultimate Seed of the world's harvest, the Seed of a divine life. In the world and for the world, his is a sovereign destiny. He is not simply an example or guide, the pattern of what the world is called to: he is a seed of sovereign fertility to raise the whole harvest of the world to the height to which he, as *God* made man, was destined; he is *God* who has become, through his incarnation, the leaven of the world.

While history goes on developing, the leaven is hidden in the dough. It is working there, but this is the time of faith, of things not seen, because it is the time of human freedom. At the hour fixed by the Father, the holy Seed, having worked upon the world into which he came, will bring out the effects of his activity into the full light of day. We shall see you, Lord, coming in power and glory (Matt. xxiv. 30, xxv. 31; Luke ix. 26, xxi. 27); and you will give this world a new countenance. Having taken its face when you came in lowliness, you will give it your own when you come in glory. Your Parousia [1] will be the world's Easter, the universe that will come forth from it will be a paschal universe, and the bells of this cosmic Pasch will be the trumpets of angels: *Canet enim tuba*, 'The trumpet will sound' (1 Cor. xv. 52).

'We find our true home in heaven. It is to heaven that we look expectantly for the coming of our Lord Jesus Christ to save us; he will form this humbled body of ours anew, moulding it into the image of his glorified body, so effective is his power to make all things obey him' (Phil. iii. 21; read also Rom. i. 4, vi. 4, viii. 11; 1 Cor. xv. 20–28, 52–53).

These three major enunciations of God's word are clearly not scientific statements. It is no good looking in them for proof or confirmation or amplification of the findings of physical science. Scientists today are prepared to offer a very approximate date for the beginning of the matter of which our world is made—four or five milliard years ago. But the statement of the Bible, 'In the beginning God created heaven and earth', belongs to quite another order and is on quite a different level from physico-chemical calculations. In the same way science has its conclusions and its hypotheses about the end of the world, but those of the Bible are of a different order of knowledge and depend on other preoccupations.

---

[1] Christ's second coming, in power and glory, at the end of time: from a Greek word meaning a royal arrival.

They are essentially relative to the history of salvation, to the main, one may say the sole, content of Revelation—the truth concerning the religious relationship that God wishes to form with us. What holy Scripture says about the end of the world is not meant to satisfy our curiosity, or to frighten us like children—that is not the true God's way, he is our Father! The Bible answers Gauguin's great questions, 'Where do we come from? What are we? Where are we going?' from the central and decisive standpoint of their connexion with the truth of religious relationship; our answer must be that we come from God, that this world is wholly dependent on him, that God has a purpose for this world in which he calls us to collaborate, and that this world which is from God will return to him. The end in question here is not the end which lies in the forces of the cosmos itself, or rather in the finite character of those forces; it is the end which lies in the mighty hands of Christ, obedient to the Father's will.

We must therefore refrain from looking for some sort of 'concordism' between biblical forms of speech, *which are not scientific* and do not have to be, and the knowledge and theories of learned men, such as cooling of the earth, heating-up of the sun, collision between stars.

2. '*Tell us, when will this be?*'

We know that in the first three written gospels there are several passages which seem to suppose, or even to state, that a final consummation was imminent. There is first of all what is called the Eschatological Discourse, i.e. that which is concerned with 'the end' (Mark xiii; Matt. xxiv. 1–25, 41; Luke xxi. 5–36); and then there are a number of isolated references, of which the chief are those of St Matt. (x. 23, xvi. 27–28; Mark viii. 39; Luke ix. 27).

Here we are face to face with one of those many cases where the Bible cannot be properly understood without the help of an education in scriptural things which few men have got, or even are in the way of acquiring. One has to be familiar with many biblical themes, forms of expression and categories to see the full bearing of explanations that in a few lines can only be sketched very summarily.

Three levels or moments occur in the passages in question. Sometimes one of them takes up nearly all the picture, but the others are generally more or less present; this is because the three moments are all part of one and the same story, in which the first two herald or symbolize the last.[1] The coming of the Lord in judgement is there each time.

The three levels or moments are: (1) The siege and destruction of Jerusalem and the Temple by the Romans, a decisive event that happened in the year 70. In the history of salvation this was not only a *judgement* on the Jewish people, who had 'fallen' (Rom. xi. 11) when they in general did not accept Jesus, but also the complete elimination of the Mosaic régime, of which not one stone was left on another: this was a coming of the Lord, himself finally recognized by his followers as the one and only true Temple, the one and only sacrifice, the one and only principle of the new worship.

(2) The last coming or definitive return, when the Lord will return as the centre and spiritual principle of the world, not simply to the hearts of the faithful but to all men, undeniable in his power and his glory. Nor will his return in majesty mean judgement for his chosen people alone, but for the world and for history, because history will then be at an end. The Lord will not come again in the likeness of a slave, offered to our faith and our love, but as God (cf. Phil. ii. 6–11). He will inaugurate the new and final order of his covenant, whose tremendous design is told us in the words 'Behold, I

[1] Catholic exegesis pretty generally takes this view: P. Benoît's notes in the *Bible de Jerusalem*, Matt. xxiv and xxv; A. Feuillet in *Catholicisme*, vol. iv (1956), *s.v.* Fin du monde (he stresses the fall of Jerusalem); St Augustine, *Epist.* 197, 199, (P.L. 33, 899, 904); St Thomas Aquinas, *In IV Sent.*, d.47, q.1, a.1, qa 3, ad 2 and d. 48, s.1., a.4, qa 1, sed c.2.

make all things new!' (Apoc. xxi. 5), 'Full completion comes
after that, when he places his kingship in the hands of God,
his Father, having first dispossessed every other sort of rule,
authority and power . . ., so that God may be all in all'
(1 Cor. xv. 24, 28), 'I heard, too, a voice which cried aloud
from the throne, "Here is God's tabernacle pitched among
men; he will dwell with them, and they will be his own people,
and he will be among them, their own God. . . ." I saw no
temple in it [the new Jerusalem]; its temple is the Lord God
Almighty, its temple is the Lamb' (Apoc. xxi. 3, 22).

(3) These two comings and judgings are historical manifestations, marking historical stages. But on the plane of what
happens in *the course of history* many other comings of the Lord
take place between the year 70 and the Last Day. The New
Testament teaches us that Christ governs history: not just as
a far-away person, who will appear one day but meanwhile
is not present and not interested in what is going on, but as
actively present in this history, making of it a holy process, a
history of salvation. That is the whole meaning of the Apocalypse of St John.[1] Without any doubt there are, woven into
human history, comings of the Lord which, in the likeness of
his Pasch and his Parousia, are both a judgement on guilt and
a showing forth of his kingship: the persecutions, the barbarian invasions and the destruction of the Roman empire,
the baptism of Clovis, the deep divisions amongst Christians,
the founding of religious orders, heresies and the councils that
condemned them, the great discoveries and the new vistas
they opened up, the revolutions in France in 1789 and in
Russia in 1917, the attainment of adulthood and self-govern-
ment by peoples hitherto under paternalistic tutelage, the
oecumenical movement, and the questions these things pro-
pound for the Christian mission: there is no doubt that in all

[1] See H. M. Féret, *L'Apocalypse de S. Jean, vision chrétienne de l'Histoire*
(Paris, 1943). Eng. trans. *Apocalypse of St John* (Newman, U.S.A., 1958).

these momentous happenings there are divine judgements and comings before which our obedience in faith is called for.

That is certainly the feeling of the Church's liturgy. Whenever I have celebrated the votive Mass 'in wartime', I have always been struck by the gospel passage that is brought to our notice therein, Matt. xxiv. 3–8: '. . . you will hear tell of wars. . . . Nation will rise in arms against nation, kingdom against kingdom. . . . But all this is but the beginning of travail.' For the New Testament, this world's history is as it were one long and agonizing bringing to birth of a new world that is to be (cf. Rom. viii. 18, 22). The Lord Jesus, its Master, constantly 'comes' to it in visits that carry judgement and grace, death and life: paschal visits. And so the world's final Pasch is made ready, arduously, in the dark, with much suffering.

That, too, is the sense of the wonderful Advent liturgy; while looking forward to its fulfilment at Christmas, it does not cease to remind us of the Lord's final coming and to open our souls to all the intermediate comings in which he draws near to us and visits his people. The three comings—historically, at Bethlehem; finally, at the Last Judgement; spiritually, those of the sacred history of the world and of souls—these form a classical theme in Christian tradition: it is found in Origen in the third century, in St Bernard and Tauler in the middle ages, and again in Luther—it is common Christian property.

Throughout the centuries this feeling of imminence and expectant waiting has also taken a more dubious form, which must be properly understood. Had the work not already been done,[1] many pages of this book could be filled with references and quotations showing that in every age, not excepting our own, some people have discerned the signs and portents of the approaching end of the world. At the close of the sixth century, that great and good man Pope St Gregory I said that 'Even

[1] For example, by P. Vulliaud, *La fin du monde* (Paris, 1952), though not always with impeccable historical insight.

161

now the stars shine less brightly, and the air is becoming un-breathable.' But the stars are still shining, and the air is still good to breathe—outside those absurd and pestilential big cities! It is a well-known phenomenon, and still insufficiently studied; every disturbed era is full of apocalyptic forebodings which simple-minded or emotional people swallow whole. At such times pseudo-prophecies are revived and find fresh acceptance; and, more truthfully but regardless of true per-spective, the feeling of the impending end of all things becomes keener. One day in 1939 a Breton peasant woman said to her parish priest, 'Monsieur le Curé, this is the end of the world, isn't it?' 'I don't know about that,' he replied, 'but I do know, alas! that it will be the end of the world for many poor men!'

The end, indeed, is always imminent, it may touch the circle of our lives at any moment. The Gospel keeps on re-minding us of it: it will come like a thief in the night, at the hour when we do not expect it (cf. Matt. xxiv. 43–44 etc.; 1 Thess. v. 2–4; 2 Pet. iii. 10; Apoc. iii. 3, xvi. 15).

There is too much evidence for us to be able to deny as a fact that this or that visionary, even this or that great saint, personally believed that the Last Day was actually at hand, chronologically imminent. And there are enough texts to make us recognize that the Apostles themselves, at any rate at first, believed that Christ would return *very soon* (Thus St Paul, 1 Thess. iv. 16; 2 Cor. iv. 12, v. 3ff.). But these texts must be understood properly, and sound explanations of them are not lacking.[1] All was as if, not knowing and not stating *anything certain* by way of firm and formal judgement,[2] the Apostles had

---

[1] See J. Guitton on the distinction between mind and mentality: *La pensée moderne et le Catholicisme*, fasc. vi, pp. 191ff., fasc. ix, pp. 85ff; *Difficultés de croire* (Paris, 1948), pp. 76ff.

[2] Cf. 1 Thess. v. 2; 2 Thess. ii. 1ff., 9; these are the first of St Paul's letters and perhaps the first written documents of Christianity (in the year 51); then Matt. xxiv. 37; 2 Pet. iii. 8, 10. Where Jesus himself is concerned, the most certainly genuine passages, e.g. the Sermon on the Mount, show that he taught a morality fitted for a normal and enduring world.

for a time shared a general conviction that Christ's return was near, a conviction that depended on the 'mentality' described by Professor Guitton. This idea was simply a personal opinion, and it gradually gave way to the idea of an indefinite period of time, whose end was probably a long way off: a corresponding development of certain ideas can be seen in studying them through the succession of apostolic writings, which followed one another over some fifty years.

Apocalyptic Sects. One of the characteristics of the middle years of the twentieth century is the spread of certain sects, especially in places hitherto immune from this distemper: it is a very disturbed age, many people are thrown off their course, and American influence is far from being everywhere beneficial!

There is a certain type of mind which is disposed towards sects and finds satisfaction in them. It is characterized by the lack of reference of particular points to a whole body of thought, and by the absence of a healthy critical spirit, and consequently by credulousness. In certain sectarian environments there is a belief in diabolic manifestations and other wonders that would make the medieval chroniclers pale with envy. This second characteristic, however, is not confined to the sects; they simply provide an outlet for man's instinctive credulousness, which unhappily is sometimes able to satisfy itself within the Church herself, where everything ought to be true, intelligent and worthy of faith. But the first characteristic is more specifically theirs.

The sectarian mind is 'fundamentalist', that is, it takes the words of the Bible in a materially and rigidly literal way, taking no notice of historical conditions or literary forms; it picks out a quite small number of verses, often prophetic or apocalyptic in tone, and focuses all its attention on them; it gives a meaning to these texts without relating or harmonizing them with others, *especially with statements that are more general—* in short, it interprets them apart from the 'analogy of faith' (cf. pp. 147–8, above); it applies these prophetic and apocalyptic texts in their material sense to particular *historical* events, which it sees distinctly foretold, and it computes the material forms and the date of the occurrence of these events by means of pseudo-biblical calculations, which are really arbitrary and refutable. It is in that that the sectarian mind excels.

We will give three examples, and first the Irvingites or 'Catholic and Apostolic Church'. These followers of Edward Irving, a Scotsman, held in the nineteenth century that the Last Day was approaching, because the 'eleventh hour' had begun in 1833 and the hours are of 476 years.

Then there are the Adventists, for whom the American William Miller fixed the end of the world in 1833 itself, basing himself on Dan. viii. 14. When it became necessary to revise his calculations, he first named 22 March 1843, and then 22 October 1844 (Matt. xxv. 5–13 was invoked). When still nothing happened, a 'prophetess', Ellen G. White, explained that the 1844 date was that of Christ's enthronement in the Holy of holies. The way being then open for a further revision of the reckoning, other dates were indicated, and these found, and still find and always will find, people credulous enough to maintain them with all the strength that extreme simplicity gives to conviction.

A lot of talk is heard nowadays about Jehovah's Witnesses, otherwise the Watch Tower movement, otherwise the International Bible Students. Their founder, Charles Taze Russell, another American, announced Christ's (secret) return for 1874, and the beginning of the thousand years of peace for—1914. There would be new heavens and a new earth from 2914.

What has not been got out of the number of the 144,000 of the elect in the Apocalypse (to which Russell also appealed)? For the sectarian spirit is always also a spirit of belonging to the elect, marked by a consciousness of being 'those beyond reproach' and by a state of mind that sees themselves as the minority set apart from a world doomed to catastrophe—they will be saved in triumph!

To be Christian, one has to use one's intelligence. Of course there are 'signs of the times', and the sects' disturbing success no doubt points to the need for Catholics to take much more interest in trying to detect and read them. But the Bible's purpose is not to predict *particular* facts, as in a chronology or a description in advance. Its purpose is to tell us true things about the religious relationship, and so it directs attention rather to the great constants that are co-extensive with the whole history of salvation. Certainly these constants are expressed in particular facts, of which some represent a special and typical actualization of it (Péguy remarked that there are high points and voids, epochs and simple periods in history); but Scripture sets forth the history *as a whole,* not this or that particular fact in isolation. Think, for instance, of the number of the Beast, of the false prophets, and of the efforts made to identify these figures with *one* particular man: the numerousness of these attempts itself shows their radical inadequacy.

As for the *exact moment* of the end of the world, we must never lose sight of this peremptory principle: Passages that are obscure must be interpreted in the light of passages that are clear. *Every passage in which one might be tempted to find a precise statement or a point of departure for a calculation must give way before this absolute declaration of living Truth:* 'OF THAT DAY AND HOUR NO ONE KNOWETH.'[1] Any such computation is a will-o'-the-wisp, and moreover a playing about with this very solemn word of God.

3. *The signs that will herald the End*

The Apostles asked the Master: 'Tell us, when will this be? And what sign will be given of thy coming, and of the world being brought to an end?' (Matt. xxiv. 3). In the face of these

---

[1] Matt. ii. 36; Mark xiii. 32 (for A. Feuillet, op. cit., this refers to the fall of Jerusalem); Acts i. 7.

questions, it seems difficult to limit Jesus' reply to portents of the fall of Jerusalem, though his words can apply to that also. He mentions several signs.

(*a*) Wars, famines and cosmic disturbances, such as earthquakes, darkening of the sun and moon, disorder in the heavens. Of these cosmic signs Abbé Feuillet writes (in *Catholicisme*, vol. iv, 1956, col. 1307):

> In interpreting accounts of adversities or of the era of grace fullest allowance must be made for the pictorial and deeply symbolic language of the Scriptures. The very oriental images of cosmic turmoil are not to be taken word for word: the earth is laid waste and depopulated; it is shaken to its foundations; it reels like a drunken man, swinging like a hammock (Isa. xxiv. 1–6, 18–20); forces in the heavens disintegrate, stars fall like leaves from a vine or fig-tree (*ib.* xxxiv. 4); sun, moon and stars go dark, the moon itself becomes red as blood (Joel ii. 10, 31; Isa. xiii. 10; Ezek. xxxii. 7–8).
>
> These fanciful images, used by the prophets and popular in later apocalyptic writings (Mark xiii. 24–25, etc.; Apoc. vi. 12, viii. 5, 12, xi. 13; *Assumption of Moses* x. 4–5; *4 Esdras* v. 8, ix. 3), are nevertheless not meaningless; they are intended to denote a close link between the destiny of the universe and the destiny of man: he is viceroy of the whole creation, and when he is chastised all creation is affected (cf. Gen. iii. 17). Inversely, and for the same reason, the restoration of friendship between God and man is given a material background that is delightful: the flower-covered earth becomes a new earthly paradise, the beasts lie down together and are friendly to man (Isa. xi. 6–9, lxv. 17–25; Osee ii. 18–24; Joel iv. 18–21).

(*b*) Persecutions (Apoc. xx. 7—10; Mark xiii. 21–22). They occur at all times and wherever Christ's true followers show themselves faithful. But those which foretell that the End is near are more especially associated with 'the man of sin', 'the son of perdition' (2 Thess. ii. 3–12), 'the Beast' (Apoc. xiii) and 'Antichrist' (1 John ii. 18–22, iv. 3; 2 John vii). These texts seem sometimes to indicate an individual, sometimes a succession of individuals (cf. Mark xiii. 22), and sometimes collective intelligences that oppose the sovereignty of God and his Christ. It is very difficult to say whether this active opposition has to take an absolutely specific form, recognizable as such, when the End is actually at hand.

The final persecutions are, too, characterized as bearing more particularly on the faithfulness of true disciples, the authenticity of the faith, the deceits of false christianities (Matt. xxiv. 4; Mark xiii. 22; Apoc. xiii. 11, 17, xvi. 13, xix. 20, xx. 10).

(*c*) The clearest historical sign will be the conversion of Israel, foreseen by St Paul (Rom. xi. 11–15, 25–26) and apparently referred to by Jesus himself (Matt. xxiii. 39). Neither Paul nor our Lord give any detail of how Israel will come back, or say how long will elapse between this return and that of the Lord and the general resurrection. This sign is the most distinct, but also somewhat vague. The premonitory signs themselves will not enable men to know the day and the hour. . . .

IV   The New Earth and Our Old Planet

There is a question of the utmost importance for giving direction to the theology of earthly things and to the attitude which we, as Christians, ought to have towards *this* world, whose fashion, as St Paul wrote, will pass away. Will the new heavens and the new earth we hear about be *this present* world transfigured, or will it vanish for ever, to be succeeded by an entirely new creation?

It seems to us more and more clear and certain [1] that the aggregate of biblical passages that speak of the cosmos not only allow the first hypothesis, they require it. Looking at things with respect to Christ, it is found that the New Testa-

[1] Since our *Lay People in the Church* (London & Westminster, Ltd., 1957), pp. 77ff.

ment constantly affirms a close relation between the work of
the incarnate Word as redeemer and the work of the eternal
Word as creator. This relationship influences the Redemption
down to its final term, which is the salvation *of the world*: not
from the world, a salvation by going out of it, but this world's
(*hujus mundi*) salvation, for the benefit of the world. If we consider created things, *this* earth, *these* heavens, the Bible from
end to end affirms their close connexion and unity of destiny
with man (cf. A. Feuillet, op. cit). For the Bible, the cosmos
is a *human, historical* cosmos; it never considers it apart from
man—any more than it separates man from his place and
activity within creation—but always as involved in man's
spiritual situation. That, too, is why the messianic restoration
is always shown as having cosmic effects. One may, one
should, allow for hyperbole in the way some biblical texts
speak of it; but there remains an irreducible, unambiguous,
fundamental affirmation. Rom. viii. 19–23 is a major expression of it, but it is one amongst many; its importance cannot
be exaggerated.

Finally, what about man, *us*? On the one hand, it is certain
that it will be *we* who will rise again and find ourselves
changed (1 Cor. xv. 52). St Paul asks God to safeguard our
bodies as well as our souls to greet the coming of the Lord
(1 Thess. v. 23); he even refers to the case of those who will
be transformed without having undergone death and the
grave's corruption (*ib.* iv. 16). On the other hand, he tells us
that the new creation has already begun in the faithful, that
they are, after Christ, its firstfruits.[1]

However, we must not think of a simple renewal of what
was before, still less of a mere patching of it. The life of God's
kingdom will not be this life here, only improved and pro-
longed endlessly. Creation will be given entirely new condi-

---

[1] 2 Cor. v. 17; 2 Thess. ii. 12; Gal. vi. 15; cf. Rom. viii. 19–25; James i.
18.

tions of existence, in dependence on the perfect sway of God's Spirit over it. The Lord's Pasch is the principle of the creation, and the whole of it has to become paschal, that is, to go through a death and a resurrection: a death to the flesh (in the biblical sense of the word—the natural selfish creature) and a resurrection by the Spirit.[1] The Jesus who lives again, beyond the grave, is the same Jesus: he shows the scars of his wounds and people recognize him. And yet not the same, for the disciples do not recognize him at first sight. And so with us, it will be the same us, but changed. It will be *this* earth and *these* heavens, but they will have been regenerated, their conditions will be entirely new and very difficult for us to imagine. We do not look for the things of this present life on the other side of the veil, as did the Egyptians when they so carefully put toys with their mummified dead. It will be something very different. Yet it is emphatically *this* creation which, after having been saved, will be blessed and glorified with the children of God, who includes it in their supernatural destiny.

> Come grace, and let this world pass away.
> *Maran atha!* Come, Lord Jesus, come![2]

[1] The very biblical idea of a pasch of the world (F. X. Durwell, *La résurrection de Jésus*. Eng. trans. *Resurrection* (Sheed, London and New York, 1960); Y. M. J. Congar, *Le mystère du Temple*, pp. 235ff., 257–64) helps with such texts as 2 Pet. iii. 7, 10 and enables us to accept whatever is sound in more dramatic and pessimistic theologies, to which this passage may serve as a reference.

[2] *Didache*, 10, 6 (cf. p. 137, above); Apoc. xxii. 17, 20; 1 Cor. xvi. 22–23.

I 2

'I Believe in the Resurrection of the Body'

PAUL VALÉRY wrote:

> The dogma [that of the resurrection of the body] which
> gives to the corporal organism an importance that is hardly
> secondary, which remarkably diminishes the soul, which it
> is impossible to picture to ourselves (we are thus saved from
> ridiculousness), which goes so far as to reincarnate the body
> in order that it may share in the fullness of everlasting life,
> which is so exactly the opposite of pure spiritualism—that
> dogma sets the Church apart from most other Christian
> confessions in the most palpable way. But it seems to me
> that for the past two or three centuries no article of belief
> has been passed over more lightly in religious literature.
> Apologists and preachers hardly mention it.

We might feel inclined emphatically to protest against
these last assertions, for we have seen the restoration of an
Easter vigil, and, before and after that, a presentation of
Christianity that is centred on its paschal sun; but we have
only to look at a still recent past, to open certain books published the day before yesterday, for us to be much less inclined
to protest.

In Germany (one has to go to Germany for this kind of
work) a detailed examination has been made of eighteenth-
century catechetical and homiletic literature from the standpoint of presentation of the paschal mystery. It was found that

more attention was given to morals, to appeals to go to confession, than to proclaiming the good news of Easter and the hope it arouses in us. A Christian like Léon Bloy could make this statement—a rather disturbing one: 'I do not get any feeling of joy from the Resurrection, because for me the Resurrection never happens. I am always Jesus in agony, Jesus hanging on the cross, and I cannot see him otherwise' (*Journal*). Or again, such a work as the *Panorama du Credo*, published in 1958, has not one paragraph formally devoted to Christ's rising from the dead.

Happily there are more positive items in our balance-sheet. St Augustine was formed in a Platonic mould, but he corrected and completed his Christian thought remarkably by going to school to the Bible; and in his sermons he declares that resurrection is the most central and essential article of the Christian creed, that its denial is a blow at its most vital spot.[1] The world of antiquity, whose greatness Augustine had known and appreciated, was haunted by the desire for *immortality*. Christians are indwelt by the sure and certain hope of *resurrection*. It is a different conception of man!

Non nocet sepultura resurrecturis, the grave cannot harm those who are to rise again, wrote an eleventh-century Frenchman. We know more than one priest, more than one lay Christian, who readily admits that faith for him consists most decisively in agreeing to live his life according to the word of a Master who has promised to make him live with a never-ending life, whole and *in his body*!

CHRISTIAN CERTAINTIES. WHAT GOD'S WORD SAYS

Christian certainties are based on a fundamental certainty, the first message in the apostolic testimony: Christ is risen!

---

[1] *Enarr. in Ps.* 88, 5 (P.L., 37, 1134): *In Joan. ev.*, tr. xxiii, 6 (35, 1585); *Sermo* 361, 2 (39, 1599). Cf. Tertullian: 'Caro salutis est cardo', Salvation hinges on the flesh.

And Christ's resurrection is the principle and seed of ours.[1]
We shall rise. In *our* bodies.

Faith in the resurrection of bodies slowly emerged and was
taught in Israel (cf. Dan. xii. 2ff.; 2 Mach. vii). In the time of
Jesus, it was upheld by the Pharisees, but rejected by the
Sadducees.[2] On the other hand, when the Apostles preached it
in the Greco-Roman world they encountered pretty general
scepticism (cf. Acts xvii. 32; 1 Cor. xv. 12). There were
Epicureans, at least for practical purposes; and there were
lines of thought inspired by Plato and Pythagoras, for whom
man *consisted* in the soul: the body was a tomb or prison (a
play on the words *sôma, sema*), and death a release; a resurrection or reincarnation would have been but a new captivity.

Many or even most of the first educated Christians were
caught up in this platonizing current of spirituality. Reading
their writings today— those of the Apologists, of Tertullian,
of Augustine later—we are struck and rather moved by seeing
how God's word was too strong for them: it overcame this
mentality, which was the most lofty part of what they had
received from their world but had induced in them a too
ethereal conception of man; they did not fully associate the
body with man's highest life and with the supreme dignity of
his heavenly calling. The biblical meaning of human nature,
on the contrary, declares the unity of the human person, soul
and body. M. Merleau Ponty's phrase (which I now blame
myself for having used too easily), 'Being unto the world
through a body', is insufficient. For the Bible, man belongs to
the world, to God, to himself and to other men, not simply
'through a body', but in his body, with his body, as body.
This is the man who gave thanks to God in a hymn found in
the famous Dead Sea manuscripts, who refers to himself as

[1] Cf. Rom. viii. 10–11; Col. i. 27; Phil. iii. 21; 1 Cor. xv. 20, 23.
[2] Cf. Matt. xxii. 23 (Mark xii. 18; Luke xx. 27); Acts iv. 2, xxiii. 8.

'Him whom you made from dust with a view to the eternal gathering'.

That is why, interpreting the word of God within the historical pattern of human thought, and from time to time encountering a resurgence of spiritualism of a Platonic type, the teaching authority of the Church has emphasized the necessity of a certain exactness in the dogma of the resurrection of the body. It is not a matter of simply 're-complementing' the soul with some sort of a body from a kind of collective wardrobe; it is a matter of the recompense of my freedom, which on earth is exercised in and through a particular body, the body of my sins and of my good deeds, the body of my selfishness and my repentance, the body of my loves, of all of which it is a vehicle, even of my love of God. In the affirmation of the resurrection there is a certain requirement that it shall be *my* body.[1] But the Church's *magisterium* does not lay down either the limits of this requirement or the way in which it must be met.

HUMAN QUESTIONS. FAITH AND THE SCIENCES

Faith is faith, it stands by itself in its own order and, where it alone is concerned, without need of props or explanations. 'The vault of heaven holds up without pillars', observed Luther in this connexion. But faith exists in the mind of a believing man, and he himself lives in a certain environment, shares a culture, has contacts with other minds. Faith cannot, on this count, blame the inquiring mind for asking questions, and cannot disregard certain objections: it is a condition of its full honesty. The Christians at Corinth put several questions about the 'how' of the resurrection, and St Paul did not fail

---

[1] The so-called Athanasian Creed (Denzinger, 40); 11th Council of Toledo, 675 (Denz., 287); profession of faith of Pope Leo IX, 'Credo etiam resurrectionem ejusdem carnis quam nunc gesto' (Denz., 347); profession of faith for the Waldenses, Innocent III, 1208 (Denz., 427); 4th Council of the Lateran, 1215, 'qui omnes cum suis propriis resurgent corporibus, quae nunc gestant' (Denz., 429); etc. Several of these phrases do not imply an identity of individual 'flesh'.

to answer, in a reply that is still valid for us (1 Cor. xv. 35–58). He presents the risen body as *our body, transformed* into another and a better state. The burden of his reply is to show that one and the same thing can have different forms of existence.

But questions still remain in the mind, two especially: (*a*) What will be the conditions of existence for these risen bodies? (*b*) How is the identity of my everlasting body with my earthly body to be thought of?

(*a*) Only holy Scripture is able to give some elements of an answer to the first question, for it is a matter of which nobody has any experience; and in fact it does so, above all through what it tells us, or enables us to infer, about Christ's risen body during the forty days when he appeared to his disciples, before his personal bodily presence was to be found only in Heaven.

'Christ, now he has risen from the dead, cannot die any more; death has no more power over him' (Rom. vi. 9; cf. 1 Cor. xv. 52). Risen bodies cannot decay, they are beyond the reach of physical death and of all that leads to it. This will be so even for the bodies of those who are called to a resurrection not of life but of judgement (John v. 29), for the wicked will rise again no less than the good (Acts xxiv. 15); but only the righteous will experience the resurrection of 'sons of God', and their bodies be moulded into the likeness of the Lord's glorified body (Phil. iii. 21; Rom. vi. 5, viii. 18–23). We can, then, picture something of the state that will be theirs, and we hope ours, from what the New Testament tells us about the paschal body of Jesus Christ.

Assuredly, it is incorruptible, no longer subject to death, ageing, sickness, pain or any of the disabilities that afflict poor human bodies in this life. Jesus willed to undergo the sufferings of his passion, including that scourging which authority in those days so freely inflicted on those it despised, in order to be wholly with us before enabling us to be wholly with him.

Christ's paschal body has that perfect obedience to the spirit which the ancients called 'subtilty', a word whose old meaning is often misunderstood! It also has 'agility', independence of the weight and other restrictions that space and time impose on us. That glorified body has the shiningness, the radiance, the freshness, the beauty that Fra Angelico and Matthias Grunewald tried to paint in earthly colours, each in his own way and each knowing the undertaking was impossible.

(*b*) 'I live. I, who underwent death, am alive . . . to endless ages'; so spoke the Christ of the Apocalypse (i. 18). We shall all be able to say that one day; faith assures us that we shall —but will it be really *us*? In the soul, yes: there is no difficulty about that, for the soul is immortal, as appears expressed or implied by holy Scripture itself, whatever many Protestant writers may too readily assert.[1] But what about the body? What about those whose body has been destroyed?—Joan of Arc, whose ashes were thrown into the Seine, the 200,000 victims at Hiroshima? Where is the particle of themselves that could serve to carry that identity between the afflicted body and the glorified body that the Christian dogma seems to require? With Christ, there was no question; but what of these?

May there not be identity simply through the soul, the soul giving its identity to a body whose substance would not have belonged to the person during earthly life? It would be a little like what happens when, after an injury to the skin, it heals and its lines and whorls are remade in the pattern which is so personal to me that any policeman in the world accepts it as an unquestionable indication of my identity. Very probably, however little or much is known about it, all the cells of the human body change according to a definite rhythm; yet my

[1] The soul's life after physical death is implied, for example, in Matt. x. 28; Phil. i. 21, 23; Heb. xi. 40, compared with other texts in the same epistle; and in the Apocalypse where, from end to end, the elect live on during the continuance of earthly history.

physical identity is an undoubted fact, and one that can re-assure us somewhat. Some theologians are satisfied that the soul ensures this identity to the body; Louis Billot was one of them.

Others, among them St Thomas Aquinas, require that the resurrection body should have a minimum of the material elements which have composed the body of a given individual during his earthly life. Did the *Imago mundi* of the men of the middle ages, even when geniuses, perhaps involve notions of permanence greater than those of actual knowledge? But an Aquinas had above all an extremely high idea of God's power and causality, completely irreducible to the limits of the mechanical causality beyond which so many minds today do not go, devoted as they are simply to the sciences of measurable matter. Nothing escapes God's presence and his power. Everything can be transformed, but nothing is lost. The God who creates all that exists, the God whom nothing has ever eluded, is well able to shape a quite new creation in which nothing of the old one will be lacking.

Still, the general principles of Thomist philosophy can without difficulty be reconciled with the thesis of a bodily identity that is ensured by the soul. The body must not be thought of as something pre-existing into which the soul goes, like a tenant into a house. It is the soul that makes its body, and keeps on making it, borrowing elements from the external world, elements whose perpetual change does not prevent the maintenance of the identity of the total physical and spiritual personality which takes them over.

The reconstitution of human personalities is less a question of an integral recovery of previous elements than of giving a new explicitness to the integrating and vitalizing power of the soul. If we study it carefully, it can be seen that the identity of the body after the resurrection has nothing to do with a resuming of the molecules and cells possessed by the soul before death. The source of the identity is in the soul itself.[1]

[1] C. D. Boulogne, *Par delà la mort* (Paris, 1946), p. 210.

These questions of sacred physics seem to interest people today less than they did in the middle ages. Much more than our ancestors, we are conscious of one sole world, within which all is interchangeable. We know that this universe is composed of the same matter, from the stars in the heavens to the earth. As for the material aspect of the final resurrection, the important thing today seems less that I recover *my* body, *my* substance, than the all-embracing fact of rising again in matter of *this* world, but transfigured. We are no longer deluded into thinking, as the middle ages were in part, that we have the philosophical and scientific means enabling us to explain things that are so remote from our experience and our techniques of measurement. Everywhere there goes with our scientific knowledge a healthy consciousness of its limits: we know that it cannot lead us to any conclusion about things that it is not able to experience or measure or even picture to itself, things which depend on quite another causality from that of which science can gauge the power and explain the ways of working.

'We read of, Things no eye has seen, no ear has heard, no human heart conceived, the welcome God has prepared for those who love him' (1 Cor. ii. 9). The Gospel assures us of the reality of another world, to which Jesus is the witness, of a world *to come*, of which he is our pledge.

But not simply and solely to come. Georges Clemenceau once said bitingly, 'You can recognize an utterance of Jaurès by this—all the verbs are in the future tense.' That cannot be said of the Christian message, not even of its proclaiming of the resurrection. For when Christianity declares this triumphant hope to the world, it establishes it on asseverations whose verbs are in the past: In the beginning God created heaven and earth. Christ is risen.

In very truth he is risen!

13

Conclusion

TAKING the world as the aggregate of men and things, we say it exists through and because of God's creative power. But, once in existence, it is called to action: things flourish, the wind blows, creatures move, they walk and take hold, and so on. For each and every being, 'to do' is fully to exist.

Where man is concerned, involved in the world and in history, the activity in which he exerts his own powers and makes use of things is not subject to physical law alone: it is determined by an intention which man himself determines. Thus, to his own purely physical energies and those of the world, he adds the specifically human increment of object and meaning: this is the properly human sphere of 'values'. The problem is to know *what use* we shall make of our energies, what *meaning* we shall give to our life.

According to holy Scripture and to theological tradition as it was systematized by St Augustine especially, there is in the first place what may be called a plain being of things and of man himself, the being that represents the raw fact of their existence. But there is as it were a second level of being, precisely that of their meaning and their use. At this level, things which from the standpoint of bare existence are what they are, can become, according to whether the meaning given to them and the use made of them are or are not conformed to God, either *truly* existent or degenerate and empty—in a word, *true* or *vain*. 'Vanity', biblically speaking, is the state of a man or thing at odds with the will, and so with the pattern, of God.

But there is sin in the world, and it is active there. Egged on by the 'Powers' of which we have written earlier on, it seeks to turn man aside from following God's design. To the extent that it succeeds in this, sin subjugates man and the world to 'vanity' (cf. Rom. viii. 20). And then things or people that seem distinguished, who make a noise in the world, who are in everybody's eye, are really as empty as glistening soap-bubbles—vanity!

For the Bible, and so in accordance with the inner truth of things, earthly history is a drama: a contest between God and the evil one, the Enemy, who 'was a murderer from the beginning' (John viii. 44), an epic of perdition and deliverance. Which will win the day?

'Nothing else than the grace of God, through Jesus Christ our Lord' (Rom. vii. 25). God, the Creator, became also the Redeemer. He to whom we owe our bare existence proffers in addition the right use and the real meaning of life. By the Incarnation and the Cross he came into this world and shared our history; there he sowed new seed of life and victory—his Gospel, his Blood, his Grace, his Church, the appeal and the power of his Spirit. We are saved. We can, we must, *live like people who are saved*, the saved ones of Christ Jesus.

To live like those who are saved means, by God's grace, to give to life and to the use made of it and of the world, the meaning that God has been pleased to give them, whose chief pivots are truth, justice, love, fellowship, generousness, service of others, brotherhood, victory over that selfishness which the Bible calls 'the flesh'.

To live like Christ's saved ones means to give to life, and to the use made of it and of the world, the meaning that Jesus wills, whose secret he has confided to us in his Gospel. That is, to be true as he was true, to love as he loved, like the Servant-through-love that he willed to be. . . . And to be and do this because of him, who is the sole source of the life opened anew amidst the world and history since his Cross and our Pentecost, to carry the fruit of which to the uttermost bounds of the earth and to the end of time is the Christian mission. Until the time, that is, when Jesus Christ comes again to restore all things, having overcome death and annihilated every evil power. How much we need that return!

'Be it so, then; come Lord Jesus!

Appendix I

REINCARNATION?

THE Christian idea of salvation, with the dogma of resurrection, is absolutely contrary to the theory of metempsychosis, or better, of the reincarnation of souls. Metempsychosis signifies the change or passing of a soul from one body into another, not excluding a body of an animal; reincarnation signifies re-beginnings of life through successive births in human flesh.

Articles in works of reference give all the documentation that is needed. The only form of the theory in which we are interested here is that of certain German poets and philosophers, who argue from the conditions of moral responsibility. Fundamentally, the argument of the Origenists[1] has an analogous preoccupation: in the hypothesis of reincarnation they sought an explanation of the marked inequality amongst men, and saw in it reward or punishment for things done in a previous life. The philosophers we are referring to were thinking of the respites necessary to allow a free person time and opportunity to decide in favour of the good and to cleanse himself.

These suppositions perhaps apply a somewhat mechanical notion of moral qualification and of the reward or punishment that it deserves (a notion, incidentally, that is shared by not a few Christians). The question seems to be considered at the level of *actions*, to which sanctions are attached on a fixed scale,

[1] The more or less faithful followers of Origen (d. *c.* 254), until their condemnation in the middle of the sixth century. Their characteristic teachings were that souls, equal in origin, have been sent into bodies according to their different merits; that evil will disappear and happiness be restored to every creature (general apocatastasis); that man's freedom remains active after death.

so to speak: whereas salvation is decided at the level of the *person* and his deep inward choice of direction. Now, on the one hand, this direction can be taken just as well in one life as in a rather arbitrary series of existences; it would be the *same man* as before coming back in another body, and why should he decide otherwise than he did previously? On the other hand, the person called on to take his stand must do so in *his* body, because he is himself only when associated with *his* body, in and through *his* body: he *is* his body.

It seems to us that every theory of reincarnation springs from a false and unbiblical conception of man. It thinks of the soul as being, alone and by itself, a complete human person, and as being only *sent* into a body or into the world, from another world of souls. In our cultural tradition, such ideas derive from Platonic or Pythagorean thought, they are not native to the Bible. For Scripture, man *is* his body, the person is not complete without it. And the Bible says 'body' where we say 'active and living person': a typical example is Rom. xii. 1, where the Jerusalem Bible rightly translates St Paul's *sôma*, 'body', as 'person'.

For the Bible, a man is not a soul who *comes* into a body; he is a person who *is born* corporeally. It is true to say of the Word of God that he came into the world, because he existed before it, but even he is truly man, as he is truly God, only because he was 'born of the Virgin Mary'.

The upholders of reincarnation could invoke, wrongly, one or two biblical texts, disregarding their immediate context and the Scriptures as a whole;[1] but it would be only a subsidiary argument: the Bible is not the source of their thought. It is a philosophical construction, a mental scheme, worked out apart from the positive premises of the biblical Christian faith, to which it remains foreign.

[1] For instance, Wisdom viii. 19–20, on which see the note in the *Bible de Jérusalem*. How necessary it is to have a Bible with notes!

These positive premises include in particular the following: predestination—the only pre-existence known to holy Scripture is that which we have in the mind of God (cf., e.g. Rom. ix. 11–24, Eph. ii. 10);—man's co-operation; fundamental choice of direction of life; merit and demerit, to be followed by reward or punishment for what we have done *in the body* (2 Cor. v. 10), in our bodies, that is to say, ourselves. Unity of the person including this body which is *mine*, or better, this body which is *me*, my complete self;—new birth. Not successive births that would add nothing really new, but *one* new birth, wherein my freedom co-operates with God's grace;—after *this* life, a destiny permanently with or against God according to the choice we have made whilst in our body. But also an 'after' of our bodily existence enabling us, not indeed to repair a choice found wanting (cf. Luke xvi. 25–26), but to cleanse ourselves from the blemishes that have disfigured a right choice, Purgatory in fact;—for the after-life, the prospect of *the* resurrection. The resurrection of our bodies: a reincarnation, but in *our* flesh, and not as a new place of trial or training, but as the fullness of the glorious fellowship of our whole persons with God, in Jesus Christ who died and rose again for us.

We may add that no valid experience confirms the gratuitous and purely philosophical hypothesis of the pre-existence and reincarnation of souls. For all we know, the memories that are sometimes adduced in support are merely a matter of 'say so', or are adequately explained in some other way.

Appendix II

Has God Peopled the Stars?

Four Questions and Three Answers

THE possibility of life in other worlds is a question that crops up at short intervals. Those who raise it have not necessarily read the more popular organs of science or science-fiction, and still less need they be believers in the flying saucers that the Martians were piloting some years back. Professor Nicolay Yerusalimsky, vice-rector of the Institute of Microbiology of the Soviet Academy of Sciences, tells us that even the moon could support elementary forms of life. And suppose one day men on an interplanetary journey should meet living beings who, however different from us, show unequivocal signs of intelligence?

1. *Does God tell us about the stars?*

Is the idea of other inhabited worlds compatible with Christian teaching?

This teaching derives from Revelation, that is, from the message that God has addressed to us through his servants the prophets, the apostles, and especially through Jesus Christ. The essence of this message is contained in sacred history, the Bible. Now God has not spoken to us thus in order merely to tell us things that satisfy our curiosity. Not at all; for that purpose he has given us our reason, and the great work of that reason, of scientific research, is gradually to unravel the riddles of the universe. God has not spoken in order to tell us how many stars there are, to explain the constitution of matter, to expound the geological ages of our planet, or anything else of that kind. It is for us to work that field and find out. When God himself speaks to us, it is to tell us what we need to know about the relationship he wants us to form with him, in that we are immortal souls, made in his image and called to a life of fellowship with him, in Christ Jesus. Christian doctrine is not concerned with stars or inhabited worlds but with Heaven, which is God's temple, his house, wherein we are called to share his life.

St Augustine likens holy Scripture to a letter from our real home written to us in exile; it tells us about this home, gives us firm hope that we shall reach it one day, and instructs us on what we must do for that purpose.[1]

So, Revelation being silent on the matter, Christian doctrine leaves us quite free to think that there are, or are not, other inhabited worlds, according as we see or do not see relevant scientific pointers of weight. Biblically speaking, it is an entirely open question.

2. *Can we read between the lines?*

However, some people have found texts in which they want to see, if not formal statements, at any rate allusions which can be taken as a hint one way or the other. We knew a good priest (he bore the appropriate name of a well-known mathematical term) who saw a reference to other inhabited worlds in the parable of the Lost Sheep, where the shepherd leaves the ninety-nine of his flock and goes to look for the hundredth (Matt. xviii. 12–14; Luke xv. 4–10). The man who had a hundred sheep was the Word of God, the Good Shepherd; the sheep that strayed was mankind, fallen into sin and lost to God, for whom the Word of God left the ninety-nine others, that is, the other living beings living in other worlds. . . .

The Fathers of the Church often saw the angels in the ninety-nine faithful sheep, and mankind in the hundredth. But this interpretation is not convincing either. There is no

[1] *Enarr. in Ps.* 64, 2 (P.L. 36, 774); *Enarr.* 2 *in Ps.* 90, 1 (37, 1159).

reason for thinking of the angels in Heaven or of 'men' on other planets. We do not have to look for a meaning or a symbolism in every detail of a parable, but only for its general import. And here the meaning is clear; the gospels not only give it in the context (particularly St Luke) but in so many words: 'The Son of Man has come to save that which was lost. . . . So too it is not your heavenly Father's pleasure that one of these little ones should be lost.' The parable teaches a lesson from the shepherd's watchfulness and care, of which Jesus is the supreme example.

There is no point in being subtle about it. There is nothing in the Bible that touches the matter.

3. *What can theology say?*

But someone may persist. Granted that it cannot be said whether or not there are other inhabited worlds, yet surely theology ought to have some idea about what could be the spiritual condition of these other beings, if they do exist. After all, theology is a science, the science of God revealed; and there seems no reason why it should be loath to argue, from the data of Revelation and with the help of the 'analogy of faith' (p. 147–8, above), as other sciences do, within an hypothesis it would put forward, without, of course, pre-judging the actual reality.

Very well; since we are forced to, let us take the hypothesis.

It is possible that other worlds are inhabited by living creatures—there is no harm in thinking of Saint Exupéry's 'Asteroid B 612'. Theology does not see any difficulty about that. And science? No doubt it would be rather difficult to suppose it for the stars; but, some say, it is not without likelihood for certain planets.

The only certainty that theology contributes here is that, if living beings endowed with understanding exist elsewhere, they too are in God's image, for he is the creator and master of Mars or Venus just as he is of the Earth. They would, then, have a natural religion analogous to ours, though in forms that we cannot imagine. We say 'analogous' in order to allow for the unknown forms of their spiritual life, the particular way in which they would think and express themselves. But, in the name of the universality of truth and of mind that lives by it, it is desirable to emphasize this soul-stirring fact: in whatever forms they were expressed, the affirmations of these intelligences would refer to identically the same God as do ours and in their spiritual content would be really identical with them. Monotheism implies that. There is only one God, a supreme and absolutely first Being, a 'Maker of all things, visible and invisible', as we sing in the Creed. Absolutely speaking, even philosophically speaking, there is only one Universe, a sole aggregate of created things, because, whatever the distribution and arrangement of these things, they all are dependent on God's design, even if the realization of it is broken up into parts.

As for the question whether, if these beings exist, they also would have been called by God to the life of grace and a supernatural revelation, no other answer can be given than this: 'It is possible.' Why not? But we know nothing whatever about it: it belongs to the realm of God's inviolable and sovereign freedom.

Could there have been an Incarnation in one of these inhabited worlds? Could the Word of God have taken flesh there and become a Martian, for instance, as we know that he became a man of this earth in Jesus Christ, brother of us sinful children of Adam? Or could the Father have been incarnated there, or the Holy Spirit?

St Paul tells us that we must be 'wise unto sobriety', and this is the moment to remember it, for we are beginning to ask questions that encroach on a sphere which God reserves to himself. Still, arguing from what we know by revelation about the incarnation of the Word in Jesus Christ, theologians think it is not contradictory, and therefore it would not be impossible, that the Word of God, or one of the Persons of the Blessed Trinity, should unite himself to any creature. But that is an answer to a question of pure intellectual curiosity, one of those questions that is discussed in the Schools in order to analyse an object of study from every angle. What matters for us and concerns us vitally is that which really exists, namely, God's actual plan where we are. And for us this plan has only one name: Jesus Christ.

We therefore keep within the bounds of what Revelation tells us when it declares that from henceforth Jesus Christ—'our' Christ!—is King, and can but be King, of *all* that is created: not simply of this earth, but of the whole of God's work, of the myriads of stars shining in the vault of the heavens.

The personal and substantial union that God has brought about, in Jesus Christ, between him and the human race is the highest that it is possible to realize, short of an unthinkable pantheism. Jesus Christ is, then, at the absolute pinnacle of the whole Universe, whether existing or possible, now and for ever. He is its King, just as he is King of the angels (but he is not their Redeemer). Henceforward God reigns over the whole Universe he has created, the visible and the invisible alike, not only (if we may put it so) from the Heaven of his Godhead, but in and through the divine manhood of Jesus Christ.

What an astounding destiny for the race to which we belong!

4. *And what do you think?*

Since we have already overstepped the limits of sober inquiry, another question may be added, for, once one has begun, a little more or less does not matter. A fourth question then: What do *you* think? We have discussed the possibility of other inhabited worlds; but what are your ideas about the actual fact? . . .